Your Body and How It Works

By

BARB AND PAT WARD

COPYRIGHT © 1999 Mark Twain Media, Inc.

ISBN   10-digit: 1-58037-111-6
           13-digit: 978-1-58037-111-7

Printing No. CD–1338

Mark Twain Media, Inc., Publishers
Distributed by Carson-Dellosa Publishing LLC

Visit us at www.carsondellosa.com

Table of Contents

Table of Contents (continued)

Table of Contents (continued)

Owner's Manual: Introduction

Congratulations! You are the proud owner of a wonderful machine. It is one-of-a-kind, and you will be the only owner of this particular model. It is a fantastic machine that can do many different things. Some jobs the machine will do on its own. You do not have to think about helping it. Other jobs can only be done if you concentrate and practice with the machine. This machine is guaranteed to last for your whole lifetime, but you need to be careful with this machine. Some replacement parts are available, but they are not easy to get.

In order to get the best possible use out of your machine, and to make it last as long as possible, it is a good idea to understand all the parts of this machine. Your machine is made up of a number of systems that all work together. We will take a look at the jobs and parts of eight of the systems in this machine. If you are ready, we can begin.

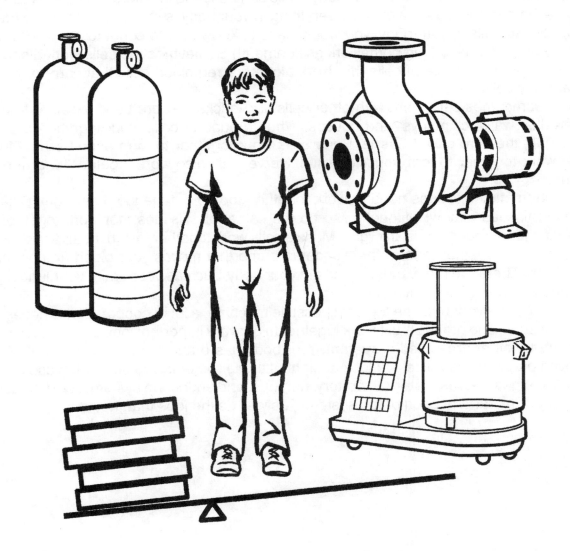

Body Organization: Working Together

Your wonderful machine is, of course, your own body. To start understanding how this "machine" works, you need to understand how your body is organized. As you know, you are a living organism. All living things have certain characteristics. One characteristic of all living things is that they are made of cells. Your body is made of trillions of very tiny cells. These cells are the building blocks of your body.

We want you to think about a brick for a minute. It is a hard, rectangular piece of matter. Bricks can be found in different shapes and sizes. You can even get bricks in different colors. A brick can be used in many different ways. One brick can be used as a door stop. Several bricks together can be used to make a sidewalk. They can be stacked to make a wall. They can be stacked even higher to make a chimney. If you have enough bricks, you can even make a house with them. For each thing that you make, the door stop, sidewalk, wall, chimney, or house, the brick is the basic unit or building block.

A cell is somewhat like a brick, except, of course, a brick is not living, but a cell is alive. A **cell** is the basic unit of your body. Cells can be found in different shapes and sizes. They even come in different colors. Everything in your body is made of cells. If you tried to count all the cells in your body, you would have to know how to count to about 70 trillion. (That would be a very long homework assignment!) Sometimes the cells work alone, like a doorstop. An example of cells that work alone are red blood cells that carry oxygen to other body cells.

Sometimes cells work with other cells, like bricks that are used together to make sidewalks, walls, chimneys, and houses. When groups of cells work together to do the same job, they are called **tissue**. Bone cells work together to form bone tissue. Muscle cells work together to form muscle tissue. Nerve cells also work together to form nerve tissue.

Sometimes tissues need to work together, too, to get the job done right. Different kinds of tissues may work together to do the same job. Tissues that work together are called **organs**. Your heart is an organ. Muscle cells work together to form heart tissue. Heart tissues work together to form the wonderful pump that moves your blood around inside your body. There are many other organs in your body, such as your brain, your lungs, your stomach, and even your skin.

To make your body be the best possible machine, a lot of cooperation is necessary. Cells, tissues, and organs must work together to get very important jobs done. These parts, working together are called a **system**. Your body has a number of systems that keep it working properly. We will take a look at eight of those systems: the skeletal, muscular, circulatory, digestive, respiratory, excretory, nervous, and endocrine systems. We will identify the important parts of each of the systems, as well as the jobs that they do.

A Graphic Organizer: Body Organization

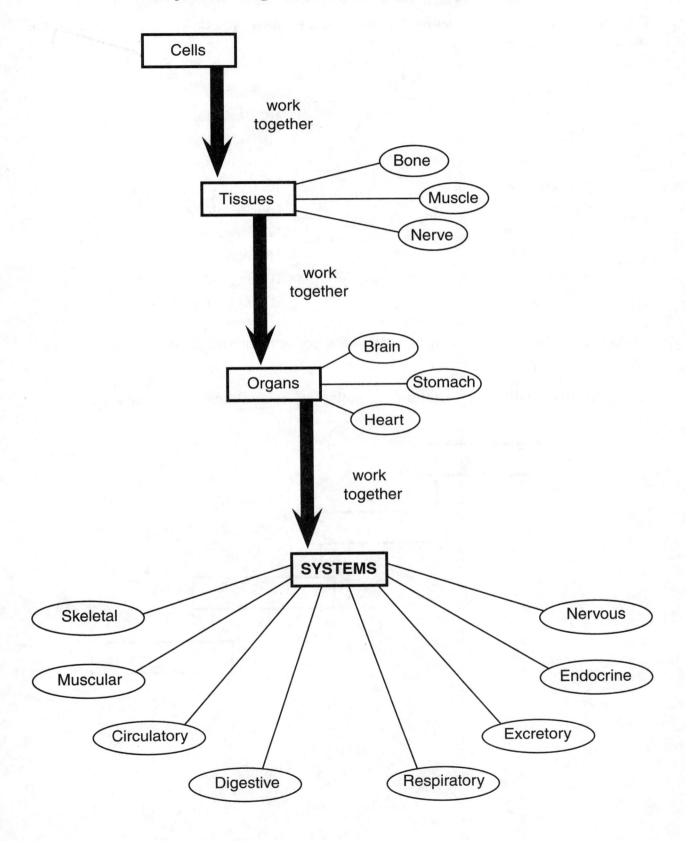

Name: _____ Date: _____

Getting It All Together: An Activity

Decide if each word represents a tissue, an organ, or a system. Write T, O, or S on the blank next to each item.

_____ 1. Kidney

_____ 2. Bone

_____ 3. Brain

_____ 4. Circulatory

_____ 5. Digestive

_____ 6. Ear

_____ 7. Endocrine

_____ 8. Excretory

_____ 9. Heart

_____ 10. Lungs

_____ 11. Muscle

_____ 12. Muscular

_____ 13. Nerve

_____ 14. Nervous

_____ 15. Nose

_____ 16. Respiratory

_____ 17. Skeletal

_____ 18. Skin

_____ 19. Stomach

_____ 20. Tongue

21. Complete the following diagram. Write the correct word from the word bank in each box.

WORD BANK: organs   cells   systems   tissues

Name: _____ Date: _____

22. Name three kinds of tissue.

    a) _____

    b) _____

    c) _____

23. Name three organs.

    a) _____

    b) _____

    c) _____

24. Name three body systems.

    a) _____

    b) _____

    c) _____

Vocabulary Review

Write a good definition for each of the following words.

1. Cell: _____

_____

2. Organ: _____

_____

3. System: _____

_____

4. Tissue: _____

_____

A Closer Look at a Human Cell

Since a cell is the basic building block of the human body, maybe we should take a closer look at a human cell. If we want to know everything possible about our wonderful "machine," we need to understand how a human cell is put together and what the different parts do.

There are four basic parts of a human cell. Beginning in the middle, the cell has a **nucleus**. The nucleus is a dense, ball-shaped part that is usually found near the center of the cell. The nucleus controls the activities of the cell. It also controls the cell's ability to reproduce. Finally, the nucleus has hereditary information in it. The nucleus of the cell has the information that determines if a person will have blue eyes or green eyes, brown hair or black hair, big feet, little hands, and so on. Sometimes, this information is called the **genes**.

All around the nucleus is the **nuclear membrane**. This membrane has the job of keeping all the parts of the nucleus inside the nucleus. We do not want genes running around where they are not supposed to be!

The next basic part of a cell is called the **cytoplasm**. This is a jelly-like material that is all around the outside of the nucleus. Cytoplasm is alive. It is made of water, salts, and other materials. Smaller cell parts, called organelles, can be found inside the cytoplasm.

The final basic part of the cell is the **cell membrane**. This membrane surrounds the entire cell. It is thin and flexible. Like the cytoplasm, the cell membrane is alive. The cell membrane keeps the cell together. It also controls movement of material in and out of the cell.

There are two kinds of movement that the cell membrane allows. The first kind of movement is called **diffusion**. Diffusion is movement from an area with many particles to an area with fewer particles. Food particles and oxygen molecules diffuse through the cell membrane into the cell. Waste products diffuse out of the cell through the cell membrane.

The other kind of movement is known as **osmosis**. Osmosis is a special kind of diffusion for fluids. Water moves through the cell membrane by osmosis.

A cell can have several smaller parts called **organelles**. The organelles are important for the life activities of the cell. They are controlled by the nucleus. One type of organelle is the **mitochondria**, which release the energy the cell needs to perform its activities. **Vacuoles** are also organelles, and they transport material through the cytoplasm in the cell. **Ribosomes** and **endoplasmic reticulum** are responsible for forming and transporting protein in the cell.

Scientists have spent a lot of time studying human cells. The study of cells is called **cytology**. Scientists have learned a lot about how cells work. However, they still have more to learn.

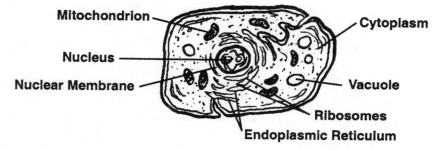

Name: _____ Date: _____

Questions

1. What is the basic unit of the human body?

_____

2. What are the four basic parts of a human cell?

_____

3. What is the job of each part you listed for question #2?

_____

_____

_____

_____

4. What is diffusion?

_____

_____

5. What is osmosis?

_____

6. What organelles are responsible for releasing energy in a cell?

_____

7. What does a vacuole do?

_____

8. What organelles are responsible for forming and transporting protein in a cell?

_____

9. What is a cytologist?

_____

10. Label the parts of the following diagram.

a. _____   d. _____

b. _____   e. _____

c. _____   f. _____

                                                       g. _____

Name: _____ Date: _____

Vocabulary Review

Write a good definition for each of the following words.

1. Cell membrane: _____

_____

2. Cytology: _____

_____

3. Cytoplasm: _____

_____

4. Diffusion: _____

_____

5. Endoplasmic reticulum: _____

_____

6. Genes: _____

_____

7. Mitochondria: _____

_____

8. Nuclear membrane: _____

_____

9. Nucleus: _____

_____

10. Organelles: _____

_____

11. Osmosis: _____

_____

12. Ribosomes: _____

_____

13. Vacuoles: _____

_____

The Framework: The Skeletal System

It is time to look closely at the first system in your wonderful machine. We will start with the skeletal system, since this provides the framework for your body. This system has three main jobs, two minor jobs, and it has four major parts. We will take a closer look at all of these jobs and parts. Let's start with the main jobs.

Three Main Jobs

To understand the first job of the skeletal system, let's think about building a house. You need to start with some wood for the framework of the house. When you put up the wood, you will know how long the house will be, how wide it will be, as well as where the windows and doors will go. You will also know how the roof will cover the house. You will know what the shape and size of the finished house will be. The wooden framework will also support the many parts of the house. It will support all the furniture and other things you put into the house, as well.

The skeletal system is similar to the wooden framework of a house. The skeletal system provides the framework for your body. It shows the size and the shape of your body. It also supports the many parts inside your body. This is the first main job of the skeletal system: **to shape and support your body**.

Now we want to understand the second job of the skeletal system, so I would like you to think about a bicycle and a car. If you are riding along the street on a bicycle, you are exposed to everything around you. If a small stone is kicked up from the road, it might hit you and hurt you. If you are riding in a car, you are not exposed to the environment. If a small stone is kicked up from the road, it might hit the hood or windshield of the car, but you will not be hurt. The car will protect you from the environment.

Inside your body, you have many parts that need to be protected from the environment. The skeletal system does that for you. Your brain is an important and sensitive organ, so it needs lots of protection. Your brain is surrounded by a hard bone known as the skull. The skull will protect your brain from damage. Your ribs and breastbone are also parts of the skeletal system. They can protect your heart and lungs. Other parts of the skeletal system are also used for protection. The second important job of the skeletal system: **to protect the organs inside your body**.

Finally, the third job is a cooperative effort. The skeletal system works with the muscular system. Together the two systems help you move your body. Some of your muscles are attached to bones in the skeletal system. When you contract or relax those muscles, the bones move up, down, forward, backward, and so on. The third main job of the skeletal system: **to work with the muscular system to move the parts of your body**.

Name: _____ Date: _____

Questions

1. How is the skeletal system similar to the wooden framework of a house?

_____

_____

_____

2. How does the skeletal system help organs inside the body?

_____

_____

_____

3. What are three organs that are protected by parts of the skeletal system?

_____

4. If the skull is supposed to protect your brain, why should you wear a helmet when riding a bicycle?

_____

_____

_____

5. What system does the skeletal system work with to help you move your body?

_____

6. What are the three main jobs of the skeletal system?

_____

_____

_____

7. What would your body look like if you did not have a skeletal system?

_____

_____

A Factory and a Storehouse

Now you have seen that the skeletal system has three very important jobs: to give shape and support, to protect organs, and to help move the body. Without the skeletal system, you would not have much of a body, would you? Now, let's take a peek at a couple of other jobs that this system performs for you.

Two Minor Jobs

In our hometown, we have a factory that makes nondairy creamer. The creamer is made in the building and then it is used by many people all around the world. They put the creamer in their coffee and enjoy a nice hot drink. Your skeletal system is like a factory. It makes blood cells. The cells move into the blood vessels and travel all around your body. Those blood cells have many important jobs to do, and you will learn more about them when you study the circulatory system. The skeletal system is responsible for **making the blood cells** so the rest of the body can use them.

We have another factory in our hometown, too. That factory makes plastic bags. Sometimes, the factory makes more bags than people need at that time. The bags are sent to a storehouse. They are kept until people are ready to buy them. Then the bags are removed from the storehouse and sent to the stores where they can be sold. Your skeletal system is also like a storehouse. When you eat, you bring minerals, such as calcium, into your body. Sometimes you eat more calcium and other minerals than you need at that time. Some of the calcium and minerals can be stored in your bones. When your body needs the calcium or minerals, it can be taken out of the bones and used by the body. Your skeletal system is also **a warehouse for fat cells, calcium, and other minerals**.

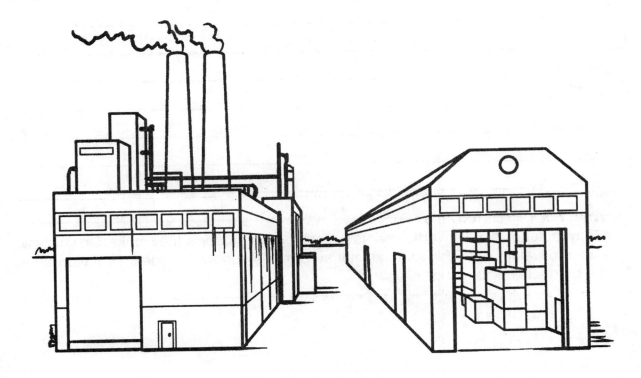

Name: _____ Date: _____

Questions

1. How is your skeletal system like a factory?

_____

_____

2. How is the skeletal system like a storehouse?

_____

_____

3. Your skeleton stores calcium. How does the calcium get into your body?

_____

_____

4. Write a good sentence using each of the following words. (Think up your own sentences, and be sure you do not just copy them from this book!)

a) skeleton: _____

_____

b) framework: _____

_____

c) factory: _____

_____

d) warehouse: _____

_____

e) protect: _____

_____

f) support: _____

_____

5. Many factories have advertisements describing the products they make. On your own paper, develop an ad for your skeletal system. Be sure to include information about the products being made!

The Thigh Bone's Connected to the ...

You have learned that the skeletal system has three major jobs and two minor jobs. There are also four basic parts to the skeletal system: the bones, the cartilage, the ligaments, and the joints. You need to understand what these parts are and how they help the system do its jobs.

First, let's study the **bones**. Just what is a bone? What are they made of? Bones are a combination of minerals, protein, water, and living matter. Two of the minerals found in bone are **calcium** and **phosphorus**. These minerals give the bones their strength and hardness. The **protein** found in bones gives them their flexibility. The living cells in the bones need some way to get food, so your bones have a blood supply as well.

Adults have about 206 bones in their bodies. All of the bones have names. Many of them have both common names and scientific names. Later, you will have a chance to learn some of the scientific names and match them to the common names.

Since you know what is in bones, you might want to know how bones are put together. Beginning at the outside of the bone, there is a protective layer or membrane called the **periosteum**. This is where the muscles are able to attach to the bones. Many bones are made of **compact bone**. This kind of tissue is very dense. It looks smooth and solid, but it is actually full of tiny tunnels called **Haversian canals**. The nerves and blood vessels that help keep the bone alive are found inside the Haversian canals. Another kind of bone tissue is called **cancellous**, or spongy bone. This is softer than the dense, compact bone. It also has nerves and blood vessels in it. Lymph tissue is found in spongy bone as well. Finally, in the center of bones there may be **bone marrow**. There are two different kinds of bone marrow. **Red bone marrow** is found in flat bones and in the ends of long bones. It is where red blood cells, white blood cells, and blood platelets are made. **Yellow bone marrow** can be found in the center of long bones and is where fat cells are stored.

Finally, bones are classified into four groups according to their shapes and functions. **Flat bones** are for protection and support. The ribs and shoulder blades are examples of flat bones. The breastbone is also classified as a flat bone. Your skeleton also has **long bones**. These bones are primarily used to support weight. Examples include your legs, arms, and your fingers. The third kind of bone is known as **short bone**. These bones are used to support weight and to allow small movements. The bones found in your ankles and wrists are short bones. Finally, there are **irregular bones** in your skeleton. The vertebrae, or backbones, are irregular bones. You also have three tiny bones in your ears that are classified as irregular bones.

Let's review what we have discussed about bones. They are made of minerals, protein, water, and living cells. There are 206 of them in the adult skeleton. Bones consist of marrow, spongy bone, compact bone, and the periosteum. Bones may be flat, long, short, or irregular in shape. WOW! No bones about it, that's a lot of new information to learn.

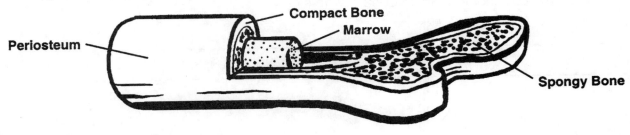

Periosteum   Compact Bone   Marrow   Spongy Bone

Name: _Grant Parks_____ Date: _9/12/16_____

Questions

1. Of what four things are bones made?

   Bones are made of minerals, protein, water and living matter.

2. How many bones are in an adult's skeleton?

   There are 206 in the adults skeleton.

3. Beginning at the inside of a bone, what are the four layers of a bone?

   In the middle there is marrow, then spongy bone, then compact bone, and on the out side is Periosteom.

4. What are the four basic shapes of bones? Give an example of each.

   There is flat bones like the pelvis, long bones like the femur, short bones like your finger bones, and irregular like your three ear bones.

5. Which type of bone is used for protection?

   Flat bones are for protection.

6. Which type of bone is used to support weight?

   Long bones support weight.

7. Which kind of bone is used for small movements?

   Short bones are used for small movements.

8. Why is it important to have calcium and phosphorus in your diet?

   Togather calcium and phosphorus provide strenth and support in your bones.

9. Why is it important to have protein in your diet?

   Protein builds and repairs tissue, and makes enzymes, hormones, hair, nails, and bones.

10. What is found inside the Haversian canals?

    Nerves and blood vessels are found in Haversian canals.

What's the Connection Here?

You have learned that the skeletal system has three major jobs. It shapes and supports the body; protects organs inside the body; and works with the muscular system to help the body move. The skeletal system also has two minor jobs to do. It makes red blood cells and stores fat cells.

The skeletal system has four basic parts: the bones, the ligaments, the cartilage, and the joints. You have learned about bones, what they are made of, how many there are in the adult body, how they are put together, how they are classified, and how they help the skeletal system do its jobs. Now, it is time to learn about ligaments and cartilage.

What is a **ligament**? A ligament is a kind of **connective tissue**. As you might guess from the word, connective tissue joins parts of the body together. Ligaments are the connective tissue that connects bones to other bones. Ligaments are tough tissue, and they are stretchy to allow bones to move. However, if you stretch a ligament too much, it can be pulled or torn. That can be very painful!

What is **cartilage**? Cartilage is another kind of tissue. It is tough like ligaments are, but it is not as stretchy. Cartilage is flexible tissue.

Cartilage can be found in many places in the body. First, cartilage is found around the ends of many bones. It is also between some of the bones at the joints where they meet. Cartilage is also found at the end of the nose and the tops of the ears.

Cartilage has three jobs. The first job is to protect bones. Cartilage acts like a shock absorber. Some cartilage is like a cushion put between the ends of bones where they meet at joints. Other cartilage is wrapped around the ends of bones.

Try a little experiment while you are sitting at your desk. Make fists with both of your hands. Imagine that your fists are the ends of your leg bones where they meet at your knees. Bounce your fists against each other several times. Imagine that you are jumping onto the ground. When you bounce your fists together this way, it might not feel very good. You would never want to jump if your legs hurt every time you tried it. Now, use two thick, soft towels or shirts. Wrap them around your hands and then bounce your fists against each other. This time it should feel better. The towels are like the cartilage that is on the ends of your bones. It protects the bones and absorbs the shocks when you move.

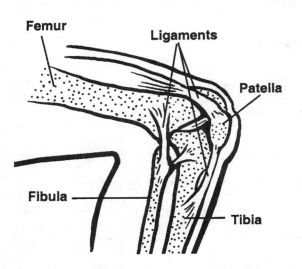

The second job of cartilage is to give shape to your body. The cartilage at the end of your nose and in your ears does that for you. Look around the room. Does everyone have the same shaped nose? Of course not, the cartilage is a little bit different for every person. That's what helps make our faces so interesting!

Finally, the cartilage in our skeletal system is to give us some flexibility. Try moving the top part of your nose, up near your eyes. You can't do it, can you? That part of your nose is solid bone. Now, try moving the tip of your nose. You can move that easily! That is the flexible cartilage that you are moving!

Name: _____ Date: _____

Questions

1. What is a ligament?

_____

2. Why is it important for ligaments to be stretchy?

_____

3. What is cartilage?

_____

4. What are three places that cartilage can be found?

_____

_____

5. Why is it important to have cartilage around the ends of bones?

_____

_____

6. You have cartilage between the bones in your spine. Why is that an important place to have cartilage?

_____

_____

7. What are the three jobs of cartilage?

_____

_____

Vocabulary Review

Write a good definition for each of the following words.

1. Cartilage: _____

_____

2. Connective tissue: _____

_____

3. Ligament: _____

_____

11/11/16

What Kind of Joint Is This?

The last part of the skeletal system is the joints. A **joint** is a place where two bones meet, or where a bone and cartilage meet. There are more than 200 bones in a human skeleton, so there are a lot of places where the bones meet. Bones have three different jobs to do. Bones must give shape and support to the body, provide protection, and work with the muscular system to help the body move. Joints can help with these jobs, especially the last one.

There are five different kinds of joints in the body. The first kind of joint is called a **fixed joint**. When the bones meet at a fixed joint, there is almost no movement. The bones are very close to each other and they stay that way. The skull is a good example of bones meeting at fixed joints. The fixed joints in your skull help protect your brain.

A second kind of joint is called a **gliding joint**. Your wrists have gliding joints. You can move your wrists back and forth. You can also move them from side to side. Try moving your back from side to side. You also have gliding joints in your backbone or spine, too.

You are able to rotate your head almost all the way around your body. You can do that because of **pivoting joints** in your neck. You can also pivot your lower arms because of the joints between those two bones.

The fourth kind of joint is called a **hinge joint**. Hinge joints allow movement back and forth, like the opening and closing of a door. Your elbows and knees are good examples of hinge joints.

Finally, a **ball-and-socket joint** allows a lot of movement. Try to make a big circle with your arm. The ball-and-socket joint in your shoulder lets you do that. Can you make a circle with your leg? You can do this because of the ball-and-socket joint at your hip.

KINDS OF JOINTS

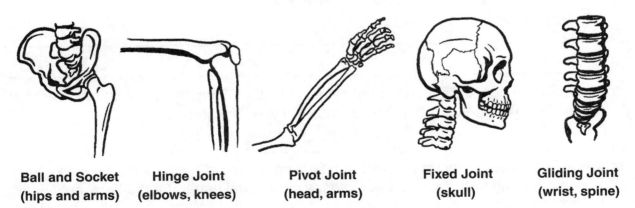

Ball and Socket   **Hinge Joint**   **Pivot Joint**   **Fixed Joint**   **Gliding Joint**
(hips and arms)   **(elbows, knees)**   **(head, arms)**   **(skull)**   **(wrist, spine)**

Name: _____ Date: _____

Questions

1. What is a joint?

_____

_____

2. What are the five kinds of joints?

_____

_____

_____

3. What is an example of each kind of joint?

_____

_____

_____

4. Which type of joint helps the skeletal system protect organs inside the body? Why?

_____

_____

5. Which kinds of joints help the body move? How?

_____

_____

6. Your pelvis is actually a group of bones held together. There is not much movement at the joints in your pelvis. What kind of joints do you think they are?

_____

7. When babies are born, they have a soft spot on the top of their head. This area allows the baby's head to fit through the mother's birth canal better. As the baby gets older, the soft spot closes up and the skull becomes more solid. Why is it important not to let a baby be hit on the head at the soft spot?

_____

_____

_____

Name: _____ Date: _____

8. Label each of the joints shown below.

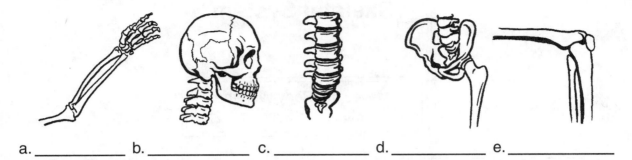

a. _____ b. _____ c. _____ d. _____ e. _____

Vocabulary Review

Write a good definition for each of the following words.

1. Ball-and-socket joint: _____

_____

2. Fixed joint: _____

_____

3. Gliding joint: _____

_____

4. Hinge joint: _____

_____

5. Joint: _____

_____

6. Pivoting joint: _____

_____

A Graphic Organizer: The Skeletal System

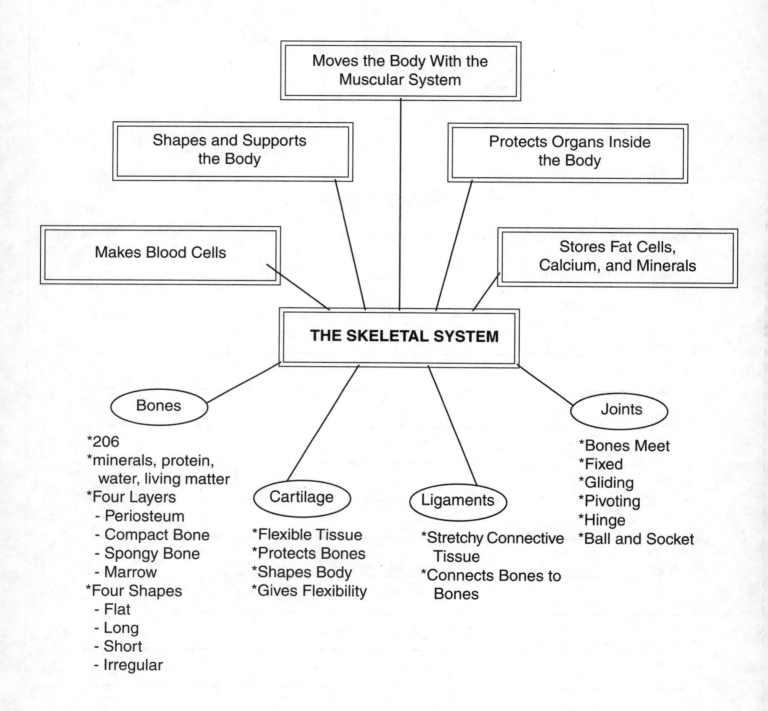

Moves the Body With the Muscular System

Shapes and Supports the Body

Protects Organs Inside the Body

Makes Blood Cells

Stores Fat Cells, Calcium, and Minerals

THE SKELETAL SYSTEM

Bones

*206
*minerals, protein, water, living matter
*Four Layers
 - Periosteum
 - Compact Bone
 - Spongy Bone
 - Marrow
*Four Shapes
 - Flat
 - Long
 - Short
 - Irregular

Cartilage

*Flexible Tissue
*Protects Bones
*Shapes Body
*Gives Flexibility

Ligaments

*Stretchy Connective Tissue
*Connects Bones to Bones

Joints

*Bones Meet
*Fixed
*Gliding
*Pivoting
*Hinge
*Ball and Socket

Things Are Changing Around Here

When you were an infant, you had a nice soft body. You were very flexible, too. Most of your body was muscle and cartilage. You did not have as much bone in your body as you do now. As you got older, your body changed. You had less and less cartilage in your body, and you had more bone to take its place.

The cartilage in your body slowly changed to make more bone. It changed in a process called **ossification**. There are four basic steps in the process of forming bone.

1. First, bone cells absorb calcium. Remember that calcium is in the foods you eat. Milk and other dairy products are good sources of calcium.

2. After the bone cells absorb the calcium, it is changed to calcium compounds. (That means the calcium joins with other elements in your body.)

3. The calcium compounds are not able to be dissolved in water, so they stay in the cells.

4. The calcium compounds harden and become bone. As the hardened bone cells are forming, the cartilage is decomposing. The body does not replace the cartilage cells with new cartilage cells, but with bone cells instead.

The process of ossification begins at birth and is usually completed between the ages of 18 and 25. It is very important to have a proper diet during this time so you can have the strongest bones possible.

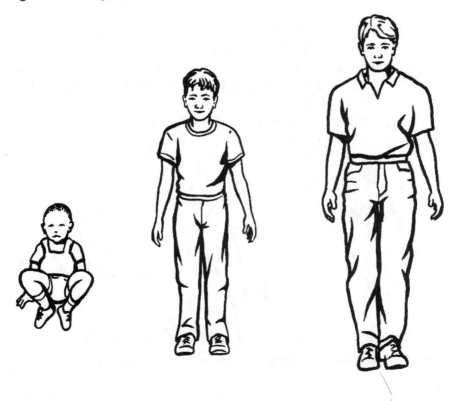

What's Your Problem?

There are times when the skeletal system does not work correctly. One kind of problem is a broken bone. A broken bone is called a **fracture**. There are several different kinds of fractures.

A **greenstick fracture** is a break in the bone. The break does not go all the way through the bone. The doctor may put a cast on the area around the fracture until it has enough time to heal. When new bone cells are made and the bone becomes strong enough, the cast can be taken off.

Another kind of fracture is called a **simple fracture**. In this case, the bone has a break all the way through it. The skin around the bone is not broken, however. The doctor may set the break, or put the pieces back together, and then put on a cast. Again, when the bone has had enough time to heal, the cast can be removed.

A third kind of fracture is known as a **compound fracture**. With a compound fracture, the bone is completely broken and the skin is broken through as well. If a compound fracture is bad enough, a doctor may have to put screws into the bone to hold it in the right place. When the bone has healed, the doctor may take out the screws. Doctors also worry about infections when there is a compound fracture. The patient may have to take powerful medicine to fight off any germs and infections.

Broken bones are not the only problems that can happen in the skeletal system. Bones can be **dislocated**. That means the bones are moved out of place. The doctor may pull the bones back into the right place. When the bones move out of place, ligaments may be torn. It can take a long time for ligaments to heal and for the injury to feel better.

Joints can have problems, too. They can become infected. **Arthritis** can be a problem in joints, especially in older people. Arthritis is an inflammation or swelling of a joint. It can be very painful!

Rickets can also be a problem. If children do not get enough calcium in their diets, their bones will not form properly. They may become very bow-legged from rickets. By adding more calcium to the diet, rickets can be cured. Remember that milk and other dairy products are good sources of calcium. Many times calcium is also added to orange juice. Check the labels on the juice containers.

Your skeletal system is very important to you. You need to do everything you can to take good care of your skeletal system.

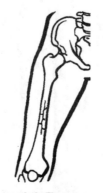
Greenstick Fracture

Simple Fracture

Compound Fracture

Name: _____ Date: _____

Vocabulary Review

Write a good definition for each of the following words.

1. Arthritis: _____

_____

2. Compound fracture: _____

_____

3. Dislocation: _____

_____

4. Fracture: _____

_____

5. Greenstick fracture: _____

_____

6. Rickets: _____

_____

7. Simple fracture: _____

_____

Steps in the healing process:

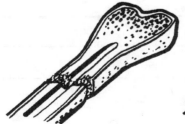  

First few days:
Spongy bone forms where the break occurs.

One to two weeks:
Blood vessels regrow between bone sections. Spongy bone fills in and hardens.

Two to three months:
The bone is almost healed.

Name: _____   Date: _____

Who Are You and What Do You Do?

There are lots of doctors and other scientists who study bones or the skeletal system. It may be confusing to try to understand what each one of them does. It may help you to know what Latin and Greek words are often used in developing English terms. For example, the Latin word for bone is *os*. The Greek word for bone is *osteon,* and the Greek word for straight is *orthos*. Use reference materials to help you develop a definition for each of the following words. Describe how each of these words relates to the skeletal system.

1. Osteology:_____

_____

_____

2. Ossify:_____

_____

_____

3. Osteopath:_____

_____

_____

4. Osteoporosis: _____

_____

_____

5. Orthopedic surgeon: _____

_____

_____

6. Orthotics: _____

_____

_____

Activities for the Skeletal System

Activity #1

Obtain a turkey bone and a beef bone. Boil both of the bones and remove any muscle tissue that remains attached to them. Cut open both bones. Have the students observe the bones and record their observations. Compare the two different kinds of bones. Help students develop hypotheses explaining the differences they have observed.

Activity #2

Divide the students into groups. Give each group an index card. Ask each group to make a bone by folding the index card in one of the following ways:

Group 1: folded like a tent
Group 2: folded in a square "tube"
Group 3: folded in a round "tube," using the short sides
Group 4: folded in a round "tube," using the long sides

Ask students to stack books on their bones. Count the number of books that each type of bone is able to support. Determine which type of bone will support the most weight. Where would the students want this type of bone in their bodies? Where wouldn't they want this type of bone in their bodies? Why?

Activity #3

Divide the students into groups. Obtain two chicken leg bones for each group. (Clean all the meat off the bones before you give them to the students.) Have the students examine the bones and record their observations. Provide each group with two jars and lids for the jars. Have the students put a bone in each jar. Have them fill one jar with water and the other jar with vinegar. Leave the bones in the jars for 24 hours and then remove the bones and rinse them well. Have the students examine the bones again, recording their observations.

The bone soaked in vinegar should be quite flexible, while the bone soaked in water should remain basically unchanged. The acid in the vinegar will react with the calcium compounds in the bone. The resulting chemical reactions will break down the calcium, leaving the bone too flexible.

Activity #4

Have students calculate the approximate weight of their bones using the following formula: weight times 35 divided by 100. What percentage of their total weight is bone? What is the weight of their bones?

Activity #5

Obtain pictures of the skeletons of animals. Compare and contrast them with a human skeleton. Review the jobs of the bones in the human skeleton. Compare the bones in the other animal skeletons. Do they have similar jobs?

Activity #6

Obtain a large beef bone. Clean off as much of the meat as possible. Have the students examine the bone, recording their observations. Be sure to measure the bone and record its weight.

Bake the bone for several hours in a medium temperature oven. Retain as much of the matter in the bottom of your baking pan as possible. When the bone has cooled sufficiently, have the students re-examine the bone. Be sure to measure the bone again and record its weight.

Help the students develop hypotheses explaining the loss of size and weight after the bone has been cooked. (Remind the students of the jobs of the skeleton, including being a warehouse for fat cells!)

Activity #7

Divide the students into groups. Give each group a clump of modeling clay, several straws, and some sheets of paper. Have the groups construct the following "bones":

1. Make a base and top out of clay. Insert the straws into the base in a random order. Add the top. Record the number of science books the bone will support.

2. Wrap the bone with a sheet of paper formed to make a cylinder. Record the number of books the bone will support now.

3. Make a base and top out of clay. Insert the straws in the base to make a cylinder. Add the top. Record the number of science books the bone will support.

4. Wrap the bone with a sheet of paper formed to make a cylinder. Record the number of books the bone will support now.

Activity #8

The adult skeleton has about 206 bones. Here is a list of the major groups of bones, the number of bones in each group and the percentage of the total number of bones in the body. Have the students develop bar graphs and circle graphs to illustrate the distribution of bones in the body.

Skull	29 bones	14%
Vertebral column	26 bones	13%
Rib cage	25 bones	12%
Shoulder	4 bones	2%
Arms and hands	60 bones	29%
Hip	2 bones	1%
Legs and feet	60 bones	29%

Research Activities

1. Compare the skeletal systems of land animals and flying animals.

2. Compare the skeletal systems of land animals and water animals.

3. Research the types of prosthetics now available. (Prosthetics are artificial limbs.) Have a specialist in prosthetics visit your classroom to demonstrate how prosthetics work. Ask the specialist to focus on the use of prosthetics by children. Have your students prepare questions ahead of time, writing them on index cards. If possible, present the questions to the specialist before the classroom visit so the discussion can focus on the areas of student interest.

4. Research the use of x-rays. Ask a radiologist to visit the classroom, bringing along sample x-rays, if possible. Again, have the students prepare questions ahead of time to help the radiologist prepare for the presentation.

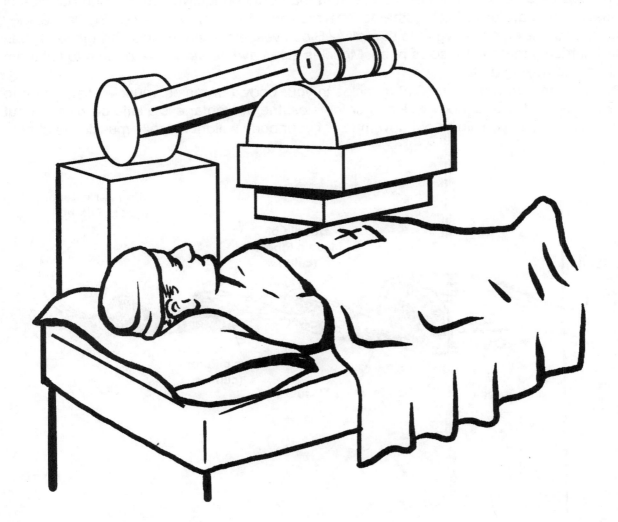

Moving Along: The Muscular System

Now that you have a better understanding of the framework for your wonderful machine, we need to figure out how the machine can move. In order to do that, we need to study the muscular system. This system has two basic jobs and two important parts that we need to look at closely. This time, let's start by looking at the parts of the system, then we can see how they work together to do their jobs.

Muscles

The first part of the muscular system that we need to learn about is the **muscles**. Muscles are organs. If you remember what you learned about the body's organization, you know that organs are groups of cells and tissues that are working together.

The basic unit of a muscle is a **muscle cell**. A muscle cell is made up of two kinds of protein filaments called **actin** and **myosin**. The actin and myosin filaments slide past each other and that makes a muscle cell work.

These muscle cells are often called **muscle fibers**. Groups of muscle fibers are wrapped together inside a special covering made of connective tissue. Then bundles of muscle fibers are grouped together to form muscles. Since muscles are living tissue, they need food, water, and oxygen to stay alive. Blood vessels in the muscles bring the oxygen and nutrients that the muscles need. Muscles also have nerve tissue in them to tell them when and how to do their jobs.

There are more than 650 muscles in your body. For males, muscles can be up to 42 percent of the total body weight. For females, the percentage is a little bit lower, about 35 percent. Can you figure out how much of your body weight is really muscle weight?

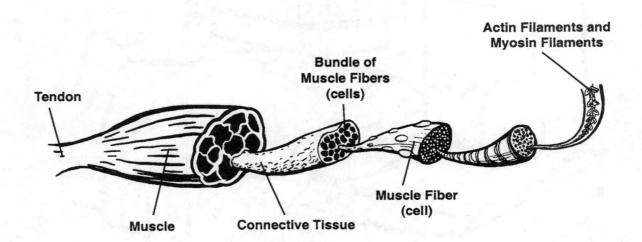

Tendon

Muscle

Bundle of Muscle Fibers (cells)

Connective Tissue

Muscle Fiber (cell)

Actin Filaments and Myosin Filaments

Name: _____ Date: _____

Questions

1. What is the basic unit of a muscle?

_____

2. What are the two kinds of protein in a muscle cell?

_____

3. What do the actin and myosin filaments do?

_____

_____

4. Why do muscles need food, water, and oxygen?

_____

5. What do nerves do for a muscle?

_____

6. How many muscles are in a human body?

_____

7. If a girl weighs 85 pounds, approximately how much of her weight is muscle?

_____

8. If a boy weighs 115 pounds, about how much of his weight is from muscles?

_____

9. Do you think that very young children and teenagers have the same percentage of muscle weight? Why or why not?

_____

Vocabulary Review

Write a good definition for each of the following words.

1. Actin: _____

2. Muscle: _____

3. Muscle fibers: _____

4. Myocin: _____

Do You Want to or Not: Classifying Muscles

Muscles are classified into two basic groups in your body: the **voluntary** muscles and the **involuntary** muscles. Let's think about those words for a minute. If the teacher asks who wants to run an errand, and you want to get out of the classroom for a few minutes, you might raise your hand. You would be *volunteering* to go for the teacher. It is something that you think about and that you want to do. Sometimes that very same teacher may tell you that you have a homework assignment. The teacher probably won't ask who wants to do it. You will probably be told that everyone must do it. It is important for you to do the homework so you can learn and move on to the next grade! You will do it *involuntarily*, but it is important for you to get it done.

Well, your muscles work in almost the same way. Sometimes there are things that you want to do. The voluntary muscles help you do them. Walking around, sitting down, jumping, running, ... the list could go on for a long time. There are other things that you have to do all the time, and your involuntary muscles do them for you. You would not be alive for long if you did not breathe and if your heart did not keep pumping. You do not even have to think about doing those things thanks to your involuntary muscles.

Some involuntary muscles can be controlled by you from time to time. Let's talk about breathing. Most of the time, you breathe without thinking. Certainly, when you are sleeping you do not have to think about breathing. Sometimes, though, you can make yourself stop breathing. You can also make yourself breathe faster or slower.

Your eyelids also have involuntary muscle action. You blink your eyes many times every day, and you probably do not really think about it. It is important to blink to keep your eyes wet. However, if you want to blink more often you can. If you want to try to stop blinking, you can stop for a while. Be careful doing that, though. It is not good for your eyes to become too dry.

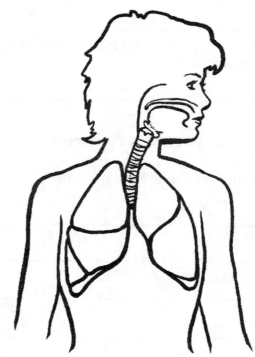

The involuntary muscles that perform the breathing process can sometimes be controlled voluntarily.

Name: _____ Date: _____

Activity

Look at the list of muscles below. Try to decide if the muscles are voluntary or involuntary. If a muscle is voluntary, write a V on the line. If a muscle is involuntary, write an I on the line. (Remember, some muscles can be both!) Good luck!

_____ 1. Arm muscles

_____ 2. Heart muscles

_____ 3. Lung muscles

_____ 4. Foot muscles

_____ 5. Small intestine muscles

_____ 6. Blood vessel muscles

_____ 7. Leg muscles

_____ 8. Hand muscles

_____ 9. Eyelid muscles

_____ 10. Bladder muscles

_____ 11. Finger muscles

_____ 12. Jaw muscles

_____ 13. Large intestine muscles

_____ 14. Throat muscles

_____ 15. Eye muscles

What Kind of Muscles Are Those?

Voluntary Muscles

Okay, now let's talk some more about those voluntary muscles. They are usually called **skeletal muscles** but sometimes they might be called **striated muscles**. If you see pictures of skeletal muscles, they look like they have stripes. That is why they are called striated muscles. Skeletal muscles look like sausages! They are long muscle fibers. They are attached to bones in the skeletal system with tendons. (We will learn more about tendons later.) Skeletal muscles need lots of oxygen and lots of nutrients so they can keep working. They have blood vessels bringing the oxygen and food to them. They also have nerves connected to them, telling them what to do and when to do it. Skeletal muscles are found in parts of your body that you can move, such as your arms, legs, hands, and face. You have more skeletal muscles than any other kind of muscle in your body.

Involuntary Muscles

There are two different kinds of involuntary muscles. First, there are the **smooth muscles** that are sometimes called **visceral muscles**. They are thin muscles with cells that look like spindles. They have the nucleus right in the middle of each cell. These muscles are connected to a special part of your nervous system called the **autonomous nervous system**. They work without you thinking about it! Smooth muscles are found in your skin, your blood vessels, and in the organs inside your body.

The other kind of involuntary muscle is very special. It is called **cardiac muscle**, and it is only found in your heart. Your heart needs a constant supply of oxygen, so cardiac muscles have lots of blood vessels. Cardiac muscles are striated like skeletal muscles, but the cells branch out and weave together so they look a little bit different. This kind of muscle acts like other involuntary muscles; you have no control over the beating of your heart. Which part of the nervous system do you think the cardiac muscles are connected to? They are controlled by the autonomous nervous system.

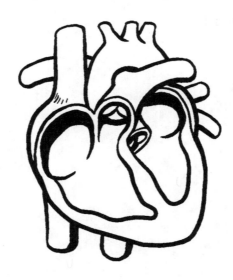

Name: _____ Date: _____

Questions

1. What are the two basic groups of muscles?

_____

2. Which muscles help you move when you want to?

_____

3. Why aren't all your body muscles voluntary muscles?

_____

_____

4. Why can your eyelid muscles be classified as voluntary or involuntary muscles?

_____

_____

5. What kind of muscles could be described as striped sausages?

_____

6. What are three places where skeletal muscles can be found?

_____

_____

7. Which part of your nervous system controls smooth and cardiac muscles?

_____

8. What do smooth muscles look like?

_____

_____

9. What are three places where smooth muscles can be found?

_____

_____

10. What is the only place where cardiac muscle can be found?

_____

_____

Name: _____ Date: _____

Vocabulary Review

Write a good definition for each of the following words.

1. Autonomous nervous system: _____

_____

_____

2. Cardiac muscle: _____

_____

_____

3. Involuntary muscle: _____

_____

_____

4. Skeletal muscles: _____

_____

_____

5. Smooth muscles: _____

_____

_____

6. Striated muscles: _____

_____

_____

7. Visceral muscles: _____

_____

_____

8. Voluntary muscles: _____

_____

_____

Holding it All Together: Tendons

When you read about the skeletal system, you learned that bones are attached to other bones by ligaments. Ligaments are special connective tissues that are stretchy, allowing bones to move. You also read that the skeletal system works with the muscular system to move the body. Well, muscles also need to be attached to the bones to get them moving.

Each muscle is attached to bone at two ends. At one end of the muscle, the attachment is firm; it does not move. This may be called the **origin** of the muscle. The muscle is attached directly to the bone at that end. At the other end of the muscle, which is called the **insertion**, the attachment can move. At that end, the muscle is attached with a connective tissue called a **tendon**.

As a muscle works, or contracts, it gets smaller. The insertion end of the muscle gets closer to the origin end of the muscle. The tendon stretches to let the muscle shorten. When the muscle relaxes, it gets longer again. The tendon shortens back to its original length. A tendon reminds me of a big, thick rubber band!

You need to be careful with your tendons, and the rest of your muscular system. If you work your muscles too hard or too suddenly without warming them up properly, you can injure yourself. The covering around the tendons may become swollen and very sore in a condition called **tendonitis**. Sometimes tendons are actually torn away from the bone where they are supposed to be attached. You may need to have surgery to fix that kind of problem! Have you ever heard of anyone having a **sprain**? A sprain is a ligament, tendon, or muscle that has been stretched too much. It can take a long time for some of these injuries to get better.

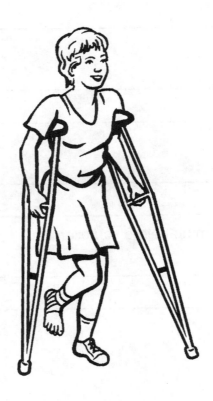

Name: _____ Date: _____

Questions

1. In how many places is a muscle attached to a bone?

_____

2. What is the origin?

_____

_____

3. What is the insertion?

_____

_____

4. What is the difference between a ligament and a tendon?

_____

_____

_____

5. Why do tendons need to be stretchy?

_____

_____

6. What is tendonitis?

_____

_____

7. What is a sprain?

_____

_____

8. Why is it important to warm up before you exercise?

_____

_____

What Kind of Job Do You Have?

Now you have studied the two important parts of the muscular system: the muscles and the tendons. Let's see what they do in your wonderful machine to keep it running smoothly.

Body Shape

One job of the muscular system is to give the body extra shape. The skeletal system provides the basic framework that decides how tall your body will be, how long your legs are, how big your head is, and so on. The muscular system provides the final shape. It decides how firm your leg muscles will be, or how round your arm muscles may look.

We all have the same basic muscles, but they do not all look the same. Our **muscle tone** is the way that our muscles look and work. Good muscle tone is developed by using muscles properly.

Think about babies. When they are born they have soft round legs. They start to kick around, and their legs get a little bit stronger. As they develop more muscle strength, they learn to pull themselves up on their legs, and then they learn to walk. When toddlers begin walking, their legs slim down, and their muscles start to show more.

Now, think about a runner on a track team. That runner spends many hours practicing and developing good leg muscles. You can see the shape of the muscles when a runner moves his or her legs. The runner has developed good muscle tone by using those muscles often. If a runner is not careful, the muscles may become too big. **Hypertrophy** is a condition in which the muscles increase in size from being used too much.

Now, think about a senior citizen. An older person may not be able to run, or even walk, as well as he or she did when younger. The muscles in the senior's legs may become softer and less noticeable. The muscles may actually become smaller. **Atrophy** is a condition in which muscles reduce in size from a lack of use.

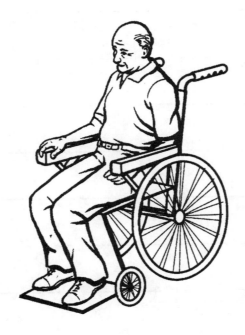

Name: _____ Date: _____

Questions

1. What gives the body its basic shape?

_____

2. What provides the final shape?

_____

3. People's muscles do not all look the same. Why is that?

_____

_____

4. What causes hypertrophy?

_____

_____

5. Why is it common for older people's muscles to atrophy?

_____

Vocabulary Review

Write a good definition for each of the following words.

1. Atrophy: _____

2. Hypertrophy: _____

3. Insertion: _____

4. Muscle tone: _____

5. Origin: _____

6. Sprain: _____

7. Tendon: _____

8. Tendonitis: _____

Which Way Are You Going?

Now you know that the muscular system is made up of muscles and tendons. You also know that it is responsible for giving your body its final shape. The other job of the muscular system is that it is responsible for moving your body parts. Your muscular system needs a little help from your skeletal system to do some of the moving.

Remember we said that you have voluntary muscles, called skeletal muscles, attached to bones in your body. How do those muscles get your bones into motion? Well, they work in pairs. One muscle in the pair starts to contract. When that muscle is done contracting, it starts to relax. The actin and myocin filaments begin sliding back, away from each other. The muscle becomes thinner and longer.

Don't forget we said that the muscles work in pairs. When one muscle is contracting, or getting shorter and thicker, the other muscle in the pair is relaxing, or getting longer and thinner. Here's a little experiment you can do to learn how muscles work in pairs. Put your right arm out at your side, straight out from your shoulder with the palm of your hand facing up. Lift your hand toward your ear, without moving your shoulder. Concentrate on the muscles in your upper arm when you move your hand. The muscle on the underside of your arm will get longer and thinner. It is relaxing. The muscle on the top of your upper arm will get shorter and thicker. It is contracting. The two muscles work together. Now put your hand back down so your arm goes straight out from your shoulder. Concentrate on the same upper arm muscles when you do that. The muscle on the top of your arm will be relaxing this time. Do you notice it getting longer and thinner? The muscle on the underisde of your arm will be contracting. You should be able to feel it getting shorter and thicker.

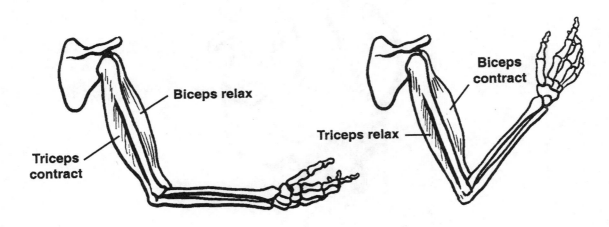

Why do your muscles move? How do they know what to do? Remember we said that your muscles are attached to nerves? Your brain sends messages through your nerves to your muscles. The nerves tell the muscles when it is time to contract and when it is time to relax. Skeletal muscles wait until you decide you want to move. You make your brain send the messages to the muscles. Skeletal muscles contract very quickly, but they tire out very quickly, too. They control your posture and your body movements.

Smooth muscles are involuntary muscles, so you do not control them directly. These muscles contract and relax slowly. Smooth muscles are responsible for pushing materials through passages in your body. For example, they push food through your digestive system. Smooth muscles also remove materials from body parts. Bile is a liquid used in the digestive system. It is expelled by smooth muscles of the gall bladder, and it is moved into the small intestines. Smooth muscles also make body openings larger and smaller. If you turn off the lights in a room, smooth muscles in your eye will make the pupil in the center of your eye larger. If you walk outside into the bright sunshine, the muscles in the eye will make the pupil very small. Finally, smooth muscles contract and restrict tubes inside your body. Smooth muscles are responsible for moving blood through the blood vessels in your body.

Cardiac muscles also contract and relax. You can feel the effects of the cardiac muscle movements if you put your finger on your pulse. (You should be able to find your pulse on your wrist or on the side of your throat.) Everyone's heart beats differently, but most of the time, hearts beat about 70 times per minute.

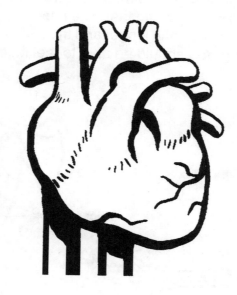

Name: _____ Date: _____

Questions

1. What happens when actin and myocin filaments begin sliding together?

_____

_____

2. Muscles work in pairs. When one muscle is contracting, what is the other muscle doing?

_____

_____

3. How do your muscles know when it is time to move?

_____

_____

4. Why do skeletal muscles tire very easily?

_____

_____

5. What are four types of movement controlled by smooth muscles?

_____

_____

_____

6. What is your pulse (definition)?

_____

_____

7. Where can you feel your pulse?

_____

_____

8. About how many times does a person's heart beat in one minute?

_____

What Class Are You In?

Your skeletal and muscular systems work together to move your body parts. Together the two systems work like a simple machine called a lever. A **lever** is defined as a bar that is used to lift weight. The bar of the lever moves on a fixed point that is called the **fulcrum**. There are three classes of levers. Let's see what they are and how they are used in the body.

First Class Lever

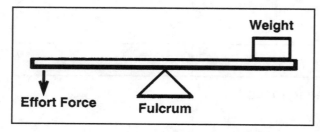

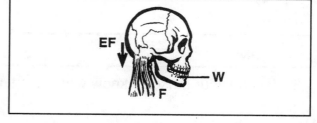

In a first-class lever, the fulcrum is in the middle, between the effort force and the weight being lifted.

If you contract the muscles at the back of your head and neck, your chin will go up into the air. The fulcrum is between the effort force and the weight.

Second Class Lever

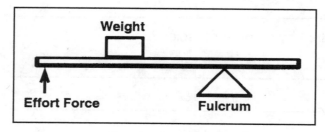

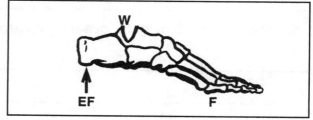

For a second-class lever, the weight is between the fulcrum and the effort force.

Stand on your toes. The weight is centered on your foot and leg, between your toes (fulcrum), and the gastrocnemius muscle (effort force.)

Third Class Lever

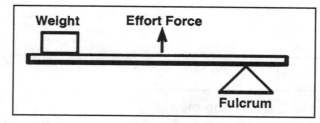

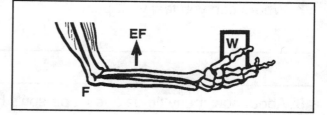

A third-class lever has yet another arrangement for the three basic parts. In this case, the effort force is between the fulcrum and the weight.

The fulcrum is your elbow, the effort force comes from the biceps muscle in your arm. The weight is your hand, forearm, container, and drink.

A Graphic Organizer:
The Muscular System

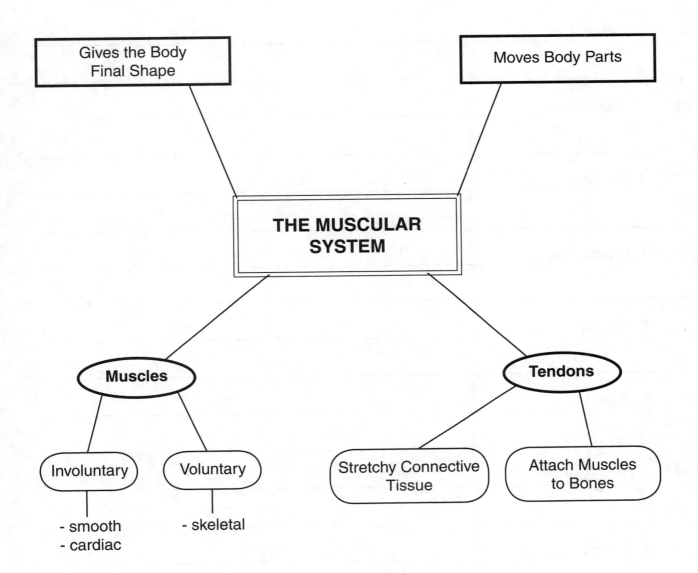

Name: _____ Date: _____

What's in a Name?

There are more than 650 muscles in the human body. The muscles all have different jobs to do and, of course, they all have different names. Look at the list of muscle names below. Using reference materials, find out what each of the muscles does. Write the job of each muscle on the line by the correct name.

1. Pectoral _____

_____

2. Intercostals _____

_____

3. Masseter _____

_____

4. Quadriceps _____

_____

5. Sternomastoid _____

_____

6. Sartorius _____

_____

7. Deltoid _____

_____

8. Triceps _____

_____

9. Biceps _____

_____

10. Gluteus maximus _____

_____

What's Your Problem Now?

You learned that there are times when the skeletal system does not work correctly. Well, the same thing is true for the muscular system. One kind of problem that many of us have had is called a **cramp**. A cramp is a painful muscle contraction. Cramps can last for quite a while as some muscles are very slow to relax. Ouch! A very severe type of contraction is called **tetanus**. Tetanus can be caused by a bacterial infection. It is a persistant contraction that won't quit. Sometimes tetanus is called lockjaw.

Another type of problem is called a **spasm**. A spasm is an involuntary contraction of a muscle. Some spasms are rapidly repeated contractions. They happen very quickly. Maybe you have had one in your eye! It sure feels funny. Very severe spasms may be called **epilepsy**. An epileptic seizure may lead to convulsions. In some cases, epilepsy can be controlled with medicine.

A **hernia** is another problem that occurs in the muscular system. Sometimes a muscle may push through into another area where it is not supposed to be. The blood will not flow normally through the herniated area, which can lead to a number of health problems. A doctor may have to surgically return the muscle to its proper place.

People do not want to have problems with any of their body sytems. To have as healthy a muscular system as possible, there are several things you can do. First of all, eat healthy foods. Your muscles need the right minerals to keep them in good working order. Your muscles also need caclium. Your body cells release calcium, and that is what gets a muscle going. Be sure you get enough protein, too. You need protein to build new muscles and to repair the ones you already have!

If you want to improve your muscle tone, you can exercise. Walking and aerobic exercises are very good for your heart muscles. Weight lifting can help shape and define muscles in your arms, legs, shoulders, back, and hips.

Finally, be sure you get enough rest. Your muscles are working hard for you all day. They need a chance to rest and rebuild. Be sure you have time to relax and be sure you get enough hours of sleep.

Name: _____ Date: _____

Questions

1. What is a muscle cramp?

_____

2. What is lockjaw?

_____

_____

3. What causes tetanus?

_____

4. What is an eye twitch?

_____

5. What is a hernia?

_____

_____

6. How are many hernias fixed?

_____

_____

7. Why would drinking milk help the muscular system?

_____

8. What kind of muscle is helped by aerobic exercises?

_____

9. What does weight lifting do for your muscles?

_____

_____

10. Why is it important to get enough sleep?

_____

_____

_____

Activities for the Muscular System

Activity #1

Divide the students into groups. Have the groups of students interview one of the following specialists.

A high school or college coach
A physical therapist
A massage therapist
A health club trainer
A sports trainer

Before conducting the actual interview, have the students prepare a set of questions. It would be helpful if all of the groups would ask similar questions in their interviews. Have the groups present their findings to the class. Compare the duties and training required for each position.

Activity #2

Obtain slides of skeletal muscle, smooth muscle, and cardiac muscle to study under a microscope. Have students record their observations, in both text and picture form.

Activity #3

1. Have students write their names 15 times on a piece of paper. Record the amount of time required to complete the activity.

2. Have students open and close their fists as many times as possible for one minute.

3. Repeat steps (1) and (2) three more times.

4. Have the students rest for five minutes and then ask them to write their names 15 more times on a piece of paper.

5. Have students answer the following questions.

How did your hand feel after the first 15 times you wrote your name?
How did your hand feel after the second 15 times?
How did your hand feel after the third 15 times?
How did your hand feel after the fourth 15 times?
How did your hand feel after you rested for five minutes?
How did your hand feel the last time you wrote your name?
Did your handwriting change? How? Why?

Activity #4

Muscles must have energy from glucose, a simple sugar, in order to contract. Carbohydrates are foods that are easily changed to glucose for the body to use. Have students develop a list of foods that are high in carbohydrates. Ask students to keep a food diary for two or three days, recording all the food they eat. Using reference materials, have the students calculate how many carbohydrate grams they have taken in during that time period.

Activity #5

Obtain one or two turkey legs for the class. Cook the legs, being careful not to pull the legs apart. Have the students observe as many structures as possible in the turkey leg. They should be able to see muscle fibers, muscle bundles and the protective sheaths around them. Students should note how the muscles narrow as they get closer to the point of attachment. Point out tendons for the students. Carefully pull the leg apart and have students continue their observations using hand lenses. Be sure to record all their observations.

It's Time to Deliver: The Circulatory System

Okay, we have studied the framework for our wonderful machine, and we understand better how the machine moves. Now we need to learn about its delivery system. We will study the **circulatory system** next. This system has two big jobs, three smaller jobs, and has three essential parts. Let's see what big jobs are done by the body's circulatory system.

Carrying Food, Water, and Oxygen

Sometimes we are a very busy family. We have many after-school activities and appointments that keep us late after work. When we get home late, after a full day, no one wants to take the time to cook dinner. Often, we will pick up the phone and order a pizza or some Chinese food to be delivered. When the food arrives, we gobble it down and get ready to tackle the next job. The food nourishes us and lets us go about our business.

Every cell in your body has certain needs that must be met for the cells to be able to stay alive. Every cell needs food, water, and oxygen. Some cells need other materials as well. The circulatory system has the awesome task of delivering the necessary "goods" to the cells. It is a bit like the delivery person who brings us the pizza or egg fu yung that we need. The circulatory system must be set up in a way that will let it make its deliveries to every single cell. It cannot miss any cells! As we learn more about the circulatory system, you will see what a truly amazing machine your body really is.

Removing Wastes From the Cells

In our everyday activities at home, at school, and at work, we create waste. When I eat a banana for breakfast, I throw away the peel because I do not want to eat it. When I open up my mail, I throw away the envelope it came in. Just think what would happen if we kept all our waste in the house. After just a few days, it would start to pile up. Then, after a week, the garbage would start to smell, and some of the other wastes could become fire hazards. Finally, the wastes would become dangerous to our health. Fortunately, most of us have garbage men who come to haul away the trash on a regular basis. Some of us have to burn or bury trash ourselves, and some of us have to haul it to the dump ourselves.

Your body cells make wastes, too. The wastes cannot stay in the cells. They would build up and prevent the cells from doing their jobs properly. Eventually, too much waste could cause the cell to die. Fortunately, we have a system to haul away the wastes from the cells: the circulatory system. When it delivers the food, water, and oxygen to each cell, it also picks up wastes from the cells. The circulatory system carries the wastes to other parts of the body where the wastes are removed from the body.

Name: _____ Date: _____

Questions

1. How is the circulatory system similar to a paper boy?

_____

_____

_____

2. Why can't the circulatory system miss any cells when it is delivering food, oxygen, and water?

_____

_____

_____

3. How is the circulatory system like a garbage truck?

_____

_____

_____

4. What does the circulatory system do with the wastes from the cells?

_____

_____

5. What would happen if the circulatory system did not pick up wastes from some of the cells in the body?

_____

_____

6. What is the circulatory system?

_____

_____

_____

The Little Things You Do

Now you know that the circulatory system is responsible for carrying food, water, and oxygen to all of the body cells. It also has the responsiblity of removing wastes from the body cells. While the circulatory system is busy doing both of those jobs, it is doing three more small chores as well.

Maintaining Body Temperature

I have coached a basketball team. We practice in the fall, inside an old gym that does not have any air conditioning. The players and I get very warm. At the end of practice, if you look around the room, you see a lot of red faces and necks as well as bright pink arms and legs.

In the winter, we heat our home with a wood stove. We are gone most of the day, so the house is really cold when we get there at the end of the day. If you could see us watching TV before the room heats up, you would see some pale faces, white hands, and maybe even some blue lips!

Our bodies try to stay at just the right temperature. When we get too hot, tiny tubes, called **capillaries**, move up near the surface of our skin. As our blood moves through the capillaries, heat is released to the surface of our skin. The heat is then absorbed into the environment that surrounds us. We get a nice rosy glow when the blood vessels are so close to the surface.

When we are too cold, the tiny capillaries move down as far as they can into our bodies. The blood wants to stay as close as possible to our important organs. Without blood flowing near the surface, we look pale.

Fighting Disease

From time to time, most of us get sick. Sometimes we have to see the doctor and get medicine to help us get better. Sometimes, we just seem to get healthy on our own. Our circulatory system has the important job of trying to keep us healthy by fighting off diseases and infections. When we talk about the different parts of the circulatory system in detail, we will get a better idea of how this job can be done.

Carrying Chemicals

Finally, the circulatory system is responsible for delivering chemicals to different parts of the body when they are needed. Sometimes the chemicals are in the food we have been eating, the liquids we have been drinking, or the medicines we have swallowed. The circulatory system adds the chemicals to its load when it is delivering food, water, and oxygen.

Name: _____ Date: _____

Questions

1. Why do kids get red in the face when they have been running around a lot?

_____

_____

2. Why do your hands get lighter colored when they are cold?

_____

_____

3. Why is it important to wear the right kind of clothes for the weather?

_____

_____

4. If you are not feeling well, how can you get better without taking medicine?

_____

_____

5. Sometimes when we are sick, we need medicine to help us get well. Why?

_____

_____

6. Eating the right kinds of food is important for a healthy body. You need vitamins and minerals. How do the vitamins and minerals get to the right parts of your body?

_____

_____

7. Milk has lots of calcium in it. Calcium is important for many parts of your body. How does the calcium get where it is needed?

_____

_____

8. When you are sick and you need medicine to help you get better, how does the circulatory system help out?

_____

_____

Parts of the Circulatory System: Have a Heart

One of the most important parts of the circulatory system is the heart. If a person is very nice, we might say the person has a heart "as big as all outdoors." Sometimes we say that a person is so mean, they are "heartless." Of course these are just expressions. Everyone must have a heart to stay alive. Let's see what a heart is.

Organ

Your heart is an organ. It is a group of cells and tissues working together to do the jobs you have already learned about. Your heart may be the most important organ in your body. Without your heart, you would not be alive. Certainly, your heart is the hardest working organ in the body, it never stops working even for one minute during your whole lifetime!

Size

Take your hand and make a fist. (Do not hit anyone!) Take a good look at your fist. That is about how big your heart is! Your heart is almost the same shape as your fist, too. Look around the room, does everyone have the same size fist? Of course not, some fists are larger and some fists are smaller! Do all of you have the same size hearts? Of course not, some hearts are larger and some hearts are smaller.

Your heart changes size as you grow. A baby has a tiny heart, the same size as the baby's tiny fist. A grown man will have a much larger heart. Remember, your heart has to carry things all around your body. As your body grows, your heart needs to grow too, just to keep up the extra work!

Location

Your heart is in the middle of your chest. It is behind the ribs and breastbone. When you say the Pledge of Allegiance to the flag of the United States, you are supposed to put your hand over your heart. Most people put their hands over the left side of their chests. Actually, the heart is more in the middle, but it is tilted. The very bottom tip of your heart is pointed toward the left side of your body.

Parts

Your heart is a combination of several important parts. The first group of parts you should know about are the chambers of your heart. Chambers are a bit like rooms. You could say that your heart has four rooms, because you have four chambers: two upper chambers and two lower chambers. The upper chambers are called the **right atrium** and the **left atrium**. The two lower chambers are called the **right ventricle** and the **left ventricle**.

Your heart also has **valves** between the chambers. Valves are like doors that only open one way. The tricuspid valve opens from the right atrium into the right ventricle. The pulmonary valve opens from the right ventricle letting blood flow into the pulmonary artery leading out of the heart. The mitral valve opens one way from the left atrium to the left ventricle. Finally, the aortic valve lets blood flow from the left ventricle out of the heart through the aorta.

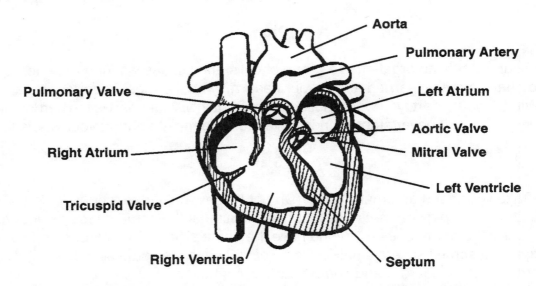

It is important for the blood on the right side of your heart not to mix with the blood on the left side of your heart. There is a thick wall of muscle between the two sides of the heart. It is called the **septum**.

Two Pumps

Remember from the skeletal system that your heart is made of special involuntary muscle. It is called cardiac muscle. The muscle in your heart works to pump your blood. Your heart is actually two pumps that work together to move your blood all around your body. One pump moves the blood from the upper chambers, or atria, into the lower chambers, or ventricles. The other pump moves the blood out of the heart and into the lungs or into the body.

When the doctor puts a stethoscope up to your chest, he or she may be listening to your heart. They want to hear the lub-dub of the pumps working. If they hear the right sounds, they can be pretty sure your heart is working correctly. The doctor may count the number of times you heart beats in one minute. If you have a good healthy heart, it should be beating between 60 and 80 times every minute. Of course, the heartbeat is different for every person, depending on the person's age, sex, and physical condition.

Name: _____ Date: _____

Questions

Read the following sentences. If a sentence is true, write LUB on the line. If a sentence is false, write DUB on the line.

_____ 1. A person can really be heartless.

_____ 2. Your heart is a group of cells and tissues working together.

_____ 3. Your heart never stops working for your whole lifetime.

_____ 4. Your heart is the same size as your fist.

_____ 5. Your heart stays the same size for your whole lifetime.

_____ 6. Everyone has the same size heart.

_____ 7. Your heart is on the left side of your chest.

_____ 8. Your heart is straight up and down in your chest.

_____ 9. Your heart has four chambers.

_____ 10. The upper chambers of the heart are called atria.

_____ 11. The lower chambers of the heart are called the septum.

_____ 12. Blood can go both ways between the atria and ventricles in your heart.

_____ 13. Valves control the flow of blood from the atria to the ventricles.

_____ 14. Valves control the flow of blood from the ventricles out of the heart.

_____ 15. The thick wall between the right and left sides of the heart is the septum.

_____ 16. Your heart is made of voluntary muscle called cardiac muscle.

_____ 17. Your heart is really two pumps.

_____ 18. One pump in your heart moves blood from the atria into the ventricles.

_____ 19. The other pump in your heart moves blood from the ventricles to the atria.

_____ 20. When a doctor hears your heart's lub-dub sounds, it means your heart is probably working properly.

Name: _____ Date: _____

Activity

Using the information from pages 55–56, label this diagram of the heart.

Word Bank:

right atrium	left atrium	right ventricle	aorta
left ventricle	pulmonary valve	aortic valve	septum
pulmonary artery	mitral valve	tricuspid valve	

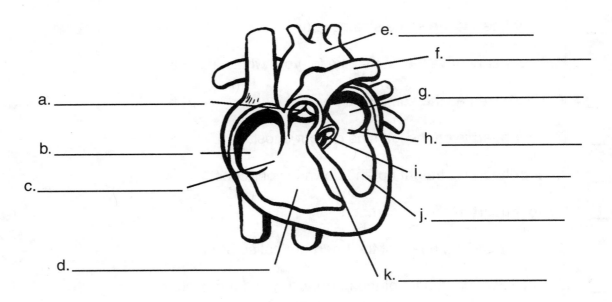

e. _____

f. _____

a. _____

g. _____

b. _____

h. _____

c. _____

i. _____

j. _____

d. _____

k. _____

Vocabulary Review

Write a good definition for each of the following words.

1. Atrium: _____

_____

2. Chamber: _____

_____

3. Septum: _____

_____

4. Valve: _____

_____

5. Ventricle: _____

_____

Parts of the Circulatory System: Tubes and More Tubes

You already know that your heart has the job of pumping your blood through your body. Your blood needs to deliver food, water, and oxygen to all of the cells. It also needs to pick up all the wastes from the body cells. To get the job done right, your circulatory system needs to have something for the blood to travel in. Your body is full of tubes for carrying the blood. There are about 95,000 kilometers of them in your body! These tubes are called blood vessels.

There are three different kinds of blood vessels in your body. Each type of vessel has a unique job to do. Let's take a look at each kind and the work it is supposed to do.

Arteries

Arteries are blood vessels that lead blood away from the heart. (Hey, that's a good way to remember: arteries go away!) These blood vessels have thick walls, but they are very elastic. They can expand and contract as the blood is pumped into them and then moves on. The arteries nearest your heart are the largest. As they get further and further from your heart, they become smaller and smaller.

Capillaries

Capillaries are the tiniest blood vessels in your body. In fact, they are so small that blood cells must go through single file. Capillaries connect the arteries with the veins. (Remember: capillaries connect!) Capillaries are thin enough to let food, water, and oxygen molecules move into them from the cells.

Veins

Veins are the third kind of blood vessel. They have the job of carrying the blood back toward the heart. Veins have thinner walls, and they look purple or blue when you see them through your skin. They are really very dark red, but we will learn more about that later.

Veins have help carrying the blood back toward the heart. If you think about your legs for a minute, it is a long way up from your foot to your heart. It would be hard to get the blood all the way up there in just one heartbeat. If veins did not have special valves in them to help control the blood flow, the blood would fall right back down into your feet! However, the valves in your veins are like the valves in your heart. They keep the blood flowing in only one direction. When the heart beats, the blood flows part of the way from your foot to your heart. Then the valves in the veins in your legs shut, blocking the blood from falling back down. With the next heartbeat, the blood can continue on its journey without losing any ground. (By the way, when you are trying to remember about veins, think veins have valves.)

Name: _____ Date: _____

Questions

1. What are blood vessels?

_____

2. How many different kinds of blood vessels are there, and what are they?

_____

_____

3. What is the job of the arteries?

_____

4. What do the capillaries do?

_____

5. Why does your body need veins?

_____

_____

6. How can the food, water, and oxygen pass from the blood vessels into the body cells?

_____

_____

7. Where would you find the largest arteries?

_____

8. How is the blood flow controlled in the veins?

_____

_____

9. Label the types of blood vessels shown in the following diagram.

a. _____

b. _____

c. _____

Parts of the Circulatory System: Blood Is Thicker Than Water

Now you know that the circulatory system carries food, oxygen, and water to all the cells of the body. It also removes waste from the body cells while it is helping the body keep the right temperature, fight disease and infection, and carry chemicals. The heart is a very important organ that pumps the blood through the body. Blood vessels are tubes that carry the blood. Finally, let's see what blood really is.

How Much Is Enough?

First of all, you have plenty of blood. Most people have about 12 pints of blood. Let's review some of our measuring skills. Two cups equal one pint. There are two pints in a quart and four quarts in a gallon, which means that there are sixteen cups or eight pints in a gallon. If you have about 12 pints of blood, that means you have about one and a half gallons of blood in your body. If you prefer to measure using liters, you have about five or six liters of blood. If you had some two-liter soda bottles, and you filled three of them, that would be about the same as the amount of blood in a body.

Once in a while, we all cut ourselves. We lose a bit of our blood. How much blood can we lose? Doctors believe that we can lose one and a half or two liters of our blood and still survive. If we lose more than that, we may not be able to keep our bodies alive.

Your blood is made up of four basic parts: plasma, red blood cells, white blood cells, and platelets. Each part of your blood looks different and has a different job to do.

Plasma

Plasma is the liquid part of your blood. Water makes up 90 percent of your plasma. Your plasma also has salts and other chemicals in it. Plasma carries dissolved foods to the cells in your body. It also carries wastes from the cells to the parts of the body that will remove the wastes. Red blood cells, white blood cells, and platelets are also found in the blood's plasma. Plasma makes up 55 percent of all your blood.

Red Blood Cells

Red blood cells make up about 44 percent of your blood. They are responsible for carrying oxygen to all the cells in your body. When they give up oxygen to the cells, they pick up carbon dioxide, a waste, from the cells and carry it to the lungs where it is removed from the body. Red blood cells are made in your bone marrow, and they are living cells. However they do not have a nucleus. Red blood cells live for about 100 to 120 days. Your bone marrow makes about $\frac{1}{2}$ cup of new red blood cells every day.

Why is your blood red? Red blood cells contain a special protein called **hemoglobin**. When hemoglobin combines with oxygen, it turns bright red. That is the color you see when you prick your finger or cut yourself and start to bleed. When hemoglobin is not combined with oxygen, it is a very dark red. It looks purple or blue when you see it through your skin and through the walls of your veins.

White Blood Cells

White blood cells make up a much smaller percentage of your blood, but they are very important cells. They are living cells with a nucleus. They are made in the spleen and in the lymph nodes. White blood cells form an army in your blood. They march through your blood vessels looking for germs to destroy. White blood cells also make antibodies. Antibodies are special chemicals that fight off specific diseases in your body.

When I was in college, I started to get very sick. The doctors were not sure what was wrong with me. They took some of my blood and counted the number of white blood cells. The number was too high. The doctors knew there was some kind of infection in my body. They did some further checking and decided to operate. They removed my enlarged and infected appendix. After the operation, I felt much better and was quickly on the road to recovery. I am very glad that my white blood cells helped the doctors figure out what was wrong with me!

Platelets

The fourth important part of your blood is called the platelets. Together with white blood cells, platelets make up the final one percent of your blood. Platelets are formed from bone cells in your bone marrow. They are not living cells. Platelets help your blood clot.

If you cut yourself, you will bleed. You do not want to lose too much of your blood. Platelets rush to the cut and use a special protein called **fibrin** to start making a special net. The net traps cells and makes a blood clot. The clot gets large enough to stop the bleeding, and then it makes a scab. After a while, the scab dries up and falls off. The cut is healed, and your blood can continue to do all of its important jobs.

Have you ever had a bruise? Do you know what it is? A bruise is actually made from blood clotting under the skin. Remember that you have lots of tiny capillaries. If you bump into a table or chair, the tiny capillaries under your skin may break open. You might have a little bleeding under the skin. The platelets rush in and make the blood clot. Then you notice a bruise. After a while, the injured area heals up and the bruise goes away.

You know it is important to get lots of calcium to keep your teeth and bones strong. It is also important for your blood. Platelets need calcium to be able to clot your blood. Calcium, of course, is found in milk and other dairy products. Keep drinking milk and eating cheese. It is helping your body in many different ways.

Name: _____ Date: _____

Questions

1. How much blood do most people have?

_____

Finish the following sentences.

2. Fifty-five percent of your blood is _____ .

3. Ninety percent of your plasma is _____ .

4. Plasma will carry _____ _____ to the cells in your body.

5. Plasma also carries _____ away from the body cells.

6. _____ _____ _____ , _____ _____ _____ , and _____ are also found in the plasma.

7. Forty-four percent of your blood is _____ _____ _____.

8. Red blood cells carry _____ to the cells and pick up _____ from the cells.

9. Red blood cells are made in your _____ _____ .

10. The protein called _____ makes your blood red when it is carrying oxygen.

11. White blood cells are made in the _____ and _____ .

12. White blood cells try to destroy _____ in your body.

13. White blood cells make _____ to fight off specific diseases.

14. Platelets help your blood _____ .

15. Platelets use a special protein called _____ to help stop bleeding.

16. You should drink lots of milk because your platelets need _____ to be able to clot your blood.

What Type Are You?

We all have the same basic parts to our blood. However, we have different chemicals within our blood. One kind of chemical is called an **antigen**. Antigens are found on red blood cells. There are two basic kinds of antigens: A and B. Scientists have found that there are four types of human blood, depending on what kind of antigens are found in a person's blood.

If a person has type A blood, that person has antigen A on their red blood cells.

If a person has type B blood, that person has antigen B on their red blood cells.

If a person has both A and B antigen on their red blood cells, that person has type AB blood.

Some people do not have antigen A or B on their red blood cells. Those people have type O blood.

We said that a person can only lose about $1\frac{1}{2}$ or 2 liters of blood. If a person loses more than that, the person might die. Doctors may be able to add more blood to a person's body in a procedure called a **blood transfusion**. It is very important for the doctors to give the person the right kind of blood. If different blood types mix together, the red blood cells may clump. The blood will not be able to travel through the blood vessels properly, and the person may die. Let's see what kinds of blood can be used in a blood transfusion.

Blood Type	Can Recieve Blood From	Can Donate Blood To
AB	AB, A, B, O	AB
A	A, O	A, AB
B	B, O	B, AB
O	O	AB, A, B, O

Most people will have either type O or Type A blood. Scientists believe more than 85 percent of all people will have one of those two types of blood. That means that less than 15 percent of all people would have type B or type AB blood. Do you know your blood type? It might be very useful information in case you or someone in your family needs to have a blood transfusion.

Name: _____ Date: _____

Activity

There has been a terrible accident and several people have been injured. You are working in the hospital, taking care of the blood supply. You are low on blood, so you need some volunteers to give their blood. You check on your list of people who have given blood in the past. You find the following information.

Susan has type A blood.
Nan has type B blood.
Alan has type AB blood.
Barb has type O blood.

The injured people are rushed into the emergency room. The doctors quickly test their blood to find out what type of blood they will need. They rush the results to you.

Joanne has type O blood.
Karen has type AB blood.

Who can give blood to Karen?

Susan	☐ yes	☐ no
Nan	☐ yes	☐ no
Alan	☐ yes	☐ no
Barb	☐ yes	☐ no

Who can give blood to Joanne?

Susan	☐ yes	☐ no
Nan	☐ yes	☐ no
Alan	☐ yes	☐ no
Barb	☐ yes	☐ no

Which Way Should I Go?

We have to drive about 15 miles to get to work. We could drive the same way every day, but that gets to be a little boring. Sometimes we change the route a little. It is more interesting, and we still get to the same place in the end.

Your blood continuously moves through your body. Remember, it has the very important job of carrying the food, water, and oxygen to the body cells and removing the wastes from those cells. The blood has a special path it follows to make sure it is doing its jobs correctly. The blood cannot change the path, it must go exactly the same way every time! Let's take a closer look at the path of your blood.

If you start with the right side of the heart, the blood begins in the **right atrium**. (Remember, that is the chamber on top!) When the cardiac muscle contracts, the blood flows through the **tricuspid valve** into the **right ventricle**. With the next contraction, the blood is moved out of the right ventricle through the **pulmonary valve**. The blood travels through the **pulmonary arteries** to the lungs. You have two lungs, so part of your blood will travel to the right lung and part of it will travel to the left lung.

Your lungs are full of tiny capillaries. When your blood arrives in your lungs, it is carrying lots of carbon dioxide that it picked up as waste from the body cells. Remember that when hemoglobin is carrying carbon dioxide, it is dark red. The molecules of carbon dioxide move out of the capillaries. Fresh molecules of oxygen move into the blood. Remember that hemoglobin turns bright red when it is carrying oxygen. With the fresh oxygen supply, the blood is ready to go to all the cells in the body. It must, however, return to the heart first. The **pulmonary veins** carry the blood back to the left side of the heart.

When returning from the lungs, the blood first enters the **left atrium**. It passes through the **mitral valve** and enters the **left ventricle**. From there, the blood passes through the **aortic valve** and enters the largest artery in your body. This artery is called the **aorta**. The aorta divides into smaller and smaller arteries that carry the blood to all the cells in your body.

When the blood arrives at the individual body cells, the oxygen that was picked up in the lungs moves into the cells. Remember, the cells are supplied by tiny capillaries. The capillaries pick up carbon dioxide in exchange for the fresh oxygen. The blood that is full of carbon dioxide arrives at the heart. Blood from the upper part of the body enters the right atrium through the **superior vena cava**. Blood from the lower parts of the body enters the heart through the **inferior vena cava**.

Now we are back at the beginning. The blood goes through this circuit of paths over and over. It only takes about one minute for blood to travel the entire way through the heart, to the lungs, back to the heart, and through the body, ending up back at the heart. It takes longer to explain the whole process!

A Graphic Organizer:
The Path of Your Blood

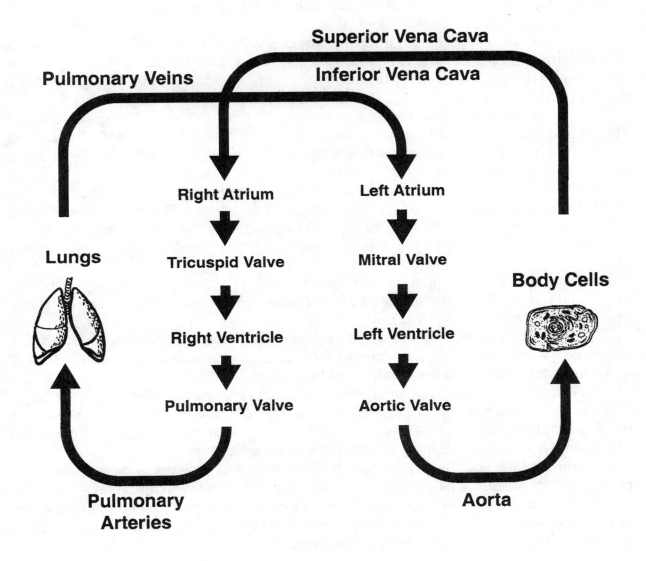

Superior Vena Cava

Pulmonary Veins   **Inferior Vena Cava**

Right Atrium   **Left Atrium**

Lungs

Tricuspid Valve   **Mitral Valve**

Body Cells

Right Ventricle   **Left Ventricle**

Pulmonary Valve   **Aortic Valve**

**Pulmonary
Arteries**   **Aorta**

There Is So Much Pressure:
Your Blood Pressure and Pulse

When I go to the doctor's office, the nurse puts a black cuff around my arm. She has a small bulb in her hand, and she pumps air into the cuff. Then she slowly lets the air out. She watches a gauge that looks like a thermometer. When she is done, she writes some numbers down on my chart. Sometimes she tells me what the numbers are. Last time, she told me my blood pressure was "120 over 80."

What does all this mean, and why would she do that to me? Well, the nurse is checking my **blood pressure**. She is seeing how much force my blood is putting on the walls of my arteries. She wants to be sure my blood is moving correctly through my body. If the pressure is not right, that could mean I have serious health problems.

The first number lets the nurse know the pressure in the arteries during a contraction of the heart muscle. Normally, this number should be between 110 and 140. The second number lets the nurse know the pressure in the arteries when the heart muscle is relaxed. This number should be between 70 and 90.

When my father went to the doctor's office, his blood pressure was too high. The doctor was worried that he might have a heart attack or a stroke. The doctor gave my dad a prescription for some medicine. The medicine helped lower his blood pressure. He has to take the medicine every day and has to have his blood pressure checked on a regular basis.

The nurse does another job to check my heart, too. She puts her fingers on the inside of my wrist. She looks at her watch and counts in her head. What is she counting, and why would she be doing that?

The nurse is feeling my artery expanding and contracting in my wrist. This happens evey time the left ventricle forces blood into the aorta. All the arteries in my body expand and contract. This is called my **pulse** or my **heart rate**.

A normal heart rate is between 65 and 75 beats in a minute, when you are resting. Your heart rate changes many times during the day. Your pulse increases when you are moving. It increases even more when you are exercising. Your pulse slows down when you are resting, and it becomes even slower when you are sleeping.

You can feel your own heart rate. If you cannot feel your pulse on your wrist, try putting two fingers on the side of your neck, right under your jaw. Push very gently and you should feel your pulse. Watch the clock and count how many times your heart beats in just one minute. Are you close to the normal heart rate? Remember, your heart rate changes depending on the activities you have been doing.

Activities for the Circulatory System

1. a. Have the students remain seated at their desks.
   b. Ask each student to find his/her pulse.
   c. Beginning on your mark, have the students count their pulse for 30 seconds and use some math skills by having them multiply by two to calculate their pulse.
   e. Have each student record his/her pulse.
   e. Repeat the above twice.
   f. Average the three results.
   g. Record the average.

2. a. Have the students run in place for two minutes and then quickly return to their seats.
   b. Beginning on your mark, have the students count their pulse for 30 seconds and use some math skills by having them multiply by two to calculate their pulse.
   c. Have each student record his/her pulse.
   d. Repeat the above twice.
   e. Average the three results.
   f. Record the average.

3. Compare the results of the resting pulse and the exercising pulse.
   a. Which pulse is higher?
   b. Why does the blood need to move more quickly during exercise?
   c. What do you think would happen if you ran in place for five minutes each time?
   d. What do you think would happen if you ran in place for 20 minutes each time?
   e. What do you think would happen if you jogged instead of ran?

Research Activities for the Circulatory System

Have each student prepare a short written or oral report about the following topics.

Cardiovascular Diseases	**Blood Diseases**	**Other**
*Arteriosclerosis	*Anemia	*Artificial Hearts
*Thrombus	*Sickle-Cell Anemia	*Electrocardiograms
*Embolus	*Leukemia	*Effects of Smoking on the Heart
*Stroke		*American Heart Association
*Hypertension		*Hereditary Factors in Heart Disease
*Hypotension		

Food for Thought: The Digestive System

Now it is time to think about the **digestive system**. Once again, we need to figure out why our bodies need this system and what all the important parts of the system are.

Fuel

First, I would like to discuss cars. I think a car is a great thing, especially if I want to get somewhere quickly. I just get in the driver's seat and turn the key to start the engine. When the car is put into gear, I can take off. I cannot go very far, however, if I do not have some fuel in the engine! I need to make sure I have enough gas in the car or I cannot get where I want to go.

Well, your body is a bit like my car. Your body needs fuel to get it going and to keep it running! Of course, you do not want to put gas into your body. You need a different kind of fuel: food. Why does your body need food? How does your body use the food you eat? Let's see if we can figure out the answers to these questions.

Food for Energy, Building, and Repairing

As you know, humans are classified as animals. More specifically, we are classified as mammals. Because of the way animals get their food, we are also classified as **consumers**. That means we need to eat plants or other animals for our food. We are not able to make our own food inside of our bodies like plants and other **producers** can!

Our bodies use the foods that we eat for three basic things. First of all, the food is used for **energy**. We need energy for the many things we do each day. We need energy to keep breathing and to keep our hearts beating. We need energy to walk, run, and jump. We also need energy to read, write, and figure out the answers to all those math questions. The busier we are, the more energy we need. Food provides us with the energy that keeps us going.

The food we eat also gives us the materials we need to build our bodies. As we grow, all the parts of our bodies grow. We need food to make new bone cells and new muscle cells. Food provides the materials that help our hair and nails grow, too. The faster you grow and change, the more food you need.

Finally, food gives us the materials we need to rebuild parts of our bodies. Think about a time you fell and hurt your knee. You probably tore off layers of skin and you may have lost some blood. The food you eat can be used to make new skin cells, fix the broken blood vessels, and replace the blood cells you lost.

Digestion

So, now you know that you need to have food. There is another problem that we need to figure out. When I am hungry in the morning, I like to eat a couple of eggs, some bacon, and some toast. How can the foods that I eat be used to make new hair cells, or new blood cells, or replace the skin cells that I scraped off yesterday when I tripped on the stairs? This is where the digestive system does its magic. The job of this amazing part of your wonderful machine is to break down the foods you eat into smaller parts that your body cells can use. The process that is used to change the food is called **digestion**. The system that digests our food is, of course, called the **digestive system**.

Name: _____   Date: _____

Questions

1. Why does your body need food?

_____

2. What would happen to your body if you did not eat for one or two days?

_____

3. What would happen to your body if you did not have any food for a long time?

_____

4. Why are people classified as consumers?

_____

5. What are four things that you do every day in school that require energy?

_____

6. Look at the list of activities below. What is happening in each activity that requires and uses energy?

   a. Playing basketball for one hour _____

_____

   b. Playing volleyball for one hour _____

_____

   c. Reading a book for one hour _____

_____

   d. Sleeping for one hour _____

_____

7. Why might young children need more food than older adults?

_____

8. What is digestion?

_____

_____

9. Why does the digestive system need to break down the food that you eat?

_____

_____

We Want This to Be as Simple as Possible!

When you sit down to a meal, you should have good food in front of you. Hopefully, you will like what you are eating. This food, however, needs to be changed into smaller parts for your body cells to be able to use it. Remember, your body needs food for energy, to build new cells, and to repair parts of your body. The food you eat is changed by the digestive system in a process called **digestion**.

There are two ways that the food you eat is changed: physically and chemically. The physical changes and the physical movement of the food through the system are called **mechanical digestion**. Let's take a look at three examples of mechanical digestion.

In your mouth, the food you eat is changed. When you chew your food, your teeth break the food into smaller pieces. Your mother is right when she tells you to chew your food well before you swallow it. Your digestive system works better when the food is broken into smaller pieces. The chewing that you do is one kind of mechanical digestion.

Mechanical digestion also takes place in your stomach. The food you swallow is combined with stomach juices. The stomach muscles mix and churn the food and the juices together. This mixing action is also an example of mechanical digestion.

When you swallow your food, mechanical digestion is taking place. Involuntary, smooth muscles are moving the food through the esophagus to the stomach. The mechanical digestion continues as your food moves through the rest of the digestive system.

When food is changed chemically, it is called **chemical digestion**. Your food is made up of nutrients. Nutrients are substances in food that you need to live and grow. The basic nutrients in your food are carbohydrates, proteins, and fats. Throughout your digestive system, you have acids, bases, and enzymes that work to change the food you eat into smaller parts and molecules. The molecules are able to travel through your body to provide you with energy, build new cells, and repair your body.

As we study all the parts of the digestive system, we will learn even more about mechanical and chemical digestion.

Name: _____ Date: _____

Questions

1. What is mechanical digestion?

_____

_____

2. What is chemical digestion?

_____

_____

Read the following sentences. If the sentence describes mechanical digestion, write M on the line. If the sentence is describing chemical digestion, write C on the line.

_____ 3. I put a banana into my mouth and I chew it.

_____ 4. My tongue moves the banana around in my mouth.

_____ 5. Saliva in my mouth starts to break down the banana.

_____ 6. My tongue pushes the banana into my esophagus.

_____ 7. The muscles in my esophagus push the banana down and into my stomach.

_____ 8. The muscles in my stomach begin to mix the banana with acids and enzymes.

_____ 9. The acids and enzymes in my stomach break the banana down more.

_____ 10. The banana/chyme mixture moves into my small intestines.

_____ 11. More enzymes, juices, and bile break down the banana/chyme mixture.

The Five Connected Parts of the Digestive System

Our digestive system is made up of five connected organs. These organs are called the digestive tract. They may also be referred to as the alimentary canal or the gastrointestinal tract. Together they measure about eight meters long. They do most of the work in breaking down your food. Several other organs help them along the way as they do their jobs.

The Beginning: Your Mouth

Okay, you are ready to eat a delicious, hot pizza. You pick up a piece and move it towards the first part of the digestive system, your **mouth**, of course! Your mouth may also be known as the **oral cavity**. In your mouth, you have a nice set of **teeth** and a rather thick muscle called a **tongue**. Your teeth are used to tear or grind your food. This is the beginning of **mechanical digestion**, breaking your food into smaller pieces. As you chew, your tongue helps you move the food around in your mouth. Your tongue also has taste buds on it, which allow you to enjoy the different flavors in your food. When your food is broken into small enough pieces, your tongue helps you swallow the food.

Along with the teeth and tongue, you have **salivary glands** in your oral cavity. These glands are hidden under your tongue. They make the saliva, or watery liquid, that you may call spit. Your saliva helps moisten the food you are eating, making it softer and easier to swallow. Your saliva is also responsible for beginning **chemical digestion**. Saliva contains enzymes, which are molecules that speed up chemical reactions. The enzymes in your mouth are called **salivary amylase**, and they help break down the starches in your food, making them into simple sugars. Scientists think you might make as much as two or three pints of saliva every day. How long would it take you to make a gallon of saliva?

The Food Tube: The Esophagus

When you swallow your food, it enters a muscular tube called the **esophagus**. This tube is about 25 centimeters long. When you are not swallowing, the esophagus flattens out. It stretches open to allow the food you have chewed to pass through it. As you swallow, involuntary muscles contract and relax, pushing your food toward your stomach. The movement created by the contracting and relaxing muscles is called **peristalsis**.

An Expandable Bag: The Stomach

Attached to the end of the esophagus is your **stomach**. This organ looks a bit like a bag, shaped like a "j." When your food enters your stomach, it mixes with **gastric juices**. These juices are enzymes, acids, and mucus. Some of the enzymes are called **pepsin**, and they help break down proteins and fats. One of the acids is known as hydrochloric acid, and it is responsible for breaking down proteins as well. The mucus in your stomach protects the stomach walls so they are not attacked by the strong acids and enzymes that are breaking down your food.

Food stays in your stomach for two to six hours. During this time, mechanical digestion takes place as the food and gastric juices are mixed together. Chemical digestion also takes place as the enzymes and acid break down the food you have eaten. When the food and juices are fully mixed, the resulting mixture is called **chyme**.

Have you ever noticed that your pants feel a lot tighter after you have eaten a big meal? Remember that we said your stomach is like a bag. Well, it is a special bag that is able to stretch. Your stomach has many folds which are able to open up and stretch out as more and more food arrives through your esophagus. When the food is broken down and begins to move out of your stomach, your pants feel more comfortable once again.

A Seven-Meter Tube: The Small Intestine

When your food has been completely mixed and churned in your stomach, it moves into your **small intestine**. The name refers to the width and not the length of this organ. In most adults, the small intestine measures about 2.5 centimeters wide and about seven meters (over 21 feet) long. It is hard to imagine such a long tube fitting into a person's body. Because the small intestine is folded many, many times like an accordian, it finds the room it needs.

The small intestine is actually a long tube that is divided into three parts; the **duodenum**, the **jejunum**, and the **ilium**. In the first section, called the duodenum, digestive juices are added to the chyme. The juices are made by the **pancreas**, the small intestine, and the liver. The juices made by the pancreas work to break down carbohydrates, proteins, and fats. The juices made by the small intestine finish the work started by the pancreatic enzymes, and they neutralize the acidity of the chyme. **Bile**, made by the **liver** and stored in the **gall bladder**, is responsible for breaking fats into smaller molecules.

In the small intestines, digestion of your food is completed. Nutrients are completely broken down into molecules that are small enough to be used by the body cells. Food moves along through this long organ by the process of **peristalsis**. This is the same process that moves food from the mouth through the esophagus to the stomach.

Just how do the molecules of food get to the body cells from the small intestine? Inside the many folds of your small intestines there are millions of **villi**. Villi are tiny fingerlike projections. These villi are surrounded by tiny blood vessels known as capillaries. Remember when you studied the circulatory system, you learned that capillaries are very thin blood vessels. The nutrients that have been broken down in the process of digestion are small enough to move out of the villi into the capillaries. They move from the digestive system into the circulatory system. Remember that one of the jobs of the circulatory system is to carry food to all the body cells. The pickup point is the small intestines!

A Two-Meter Tube: The Large Intestine

After the nutrients move from your small intestines into your blood stream, waste materials and fiber remain in your digestive system. These materials move into your **large intestine**, which is about six centimeters wide and 1.5 to two meters (around four to six feet) long. The waste materials still contain water that can be used by the body cells. Water molecules are absorbed by the blood from the large intestine. The blood carries the water along with the food to all the cells throughout the body. The remaining semisolid waste moves through the large intestine and is stored in the **rectum**. This waste material is called **feces**. When the rectum becomes full, the fecal wastes are removed from the body through the **anus**.

Name: _____ Date: _____

Activity

Look at the diagram at the right. Label the five parts of the digestive system.

a. _____

b. _____

c. _____

d. _____

e. _____

_____

Questions

1. Why do very young children need to be fed soft foods?

_____

2. Why is it important to chew your food?

_____

3. What are three jobs performed by your tongue?

_____

_____

4. Why is it easier to eat a grape than a saltine cracker?

_____

5. If you make two pints of saliva every day, how long would it take you to make a gallon?

_____

6. What is peristalsis?

_____

_____

7. What is chyme?

_____

_____

8. The small intestine is about seven meters long and the large intestine is about two meters long. Why aren't the names switched?

_____

_____

Distant Relatives:
Organs That Help the Digestive System

You have just learned that the five main organs do most of the work for the digestive system. Those organs are all connected. Beginning at the mouth, food moves through the esophagus, stomach, and small intestines before it is removed from the body through the large intestines. Other organs also play an important role in digesting your food, but they are not directly connected to the digestive tract.

Salivary Glands

First of all, you have a set of six **salivary glands**. The largest glands are called the **submaxillary glands**, and they are found under your lower jaw. The **sublingual glands** are located under your tongue, and the **parotids** are found in front of each ear. All of the salivary glands make saliva. This fluid, which we often call spit, makes your mouth wet. It also makes your food softer and easier to swallow. The saliva also begins the chemical digestion of your food as it breaks down starches into simpler sugars.

When I was a young child, I had to stay home from school for several days because I had the mumps. This was a fairly common childhood disease resulting from a virus infecting my salivary glands. I had a bit of a fever and my cheeks puffed up. I looked pretty silly. You probably will not have to worry about getting mumps, because a special vaccine was invented in 1967. The vaccine is given to young children so they will not get the mumps virus.

The Pancreas

Tucked into your body, close to your stomach, is an organ that is shaped a bit like a bunch of grapes. It is about 20 centimeters long and is about four centimeters wide. It is about 2.5 centimeters thick. This organ, the **pancreas**, has an important job to do in two different systems in your body: the endocrine system and the digestive system. For the digestive system, the pancreas makes enzymes. The enzymes are sent to the small intestines through a tube called the **pancreatic duct**. The pancreatic enzymes help your body break down carbohydrates, proteins, and fats.

The Liver

Just under your diaphragm, lying on top of your stomach, is a large red organ known as the **liver**. The liver is a very important organ, helping many of your body systems. One of the jobs the liver has is to make **bile**. Bile is a fluid containing special salts. Those salts are important for breaking down fats into smaller molecules. The bile is made in the liver and is stored in a nearby organ called the **gallbladder**. The gallbladder sends bile into the duodendum, which is the first part of the small intestine. The bile travels from the gallbladder to the small intestine through a tube called the **bile duct**.

Name: _____ Date: _____

Activity

Look at the diagrams below. Label the parts of the diagrams using the word bank.

Word Bank: submaxillary glands
sublingual glands
parotid glands
pancreas
pancreatic duct
liver
gallbladder
bile duct

a. _____

_____

b. _____

c. _____

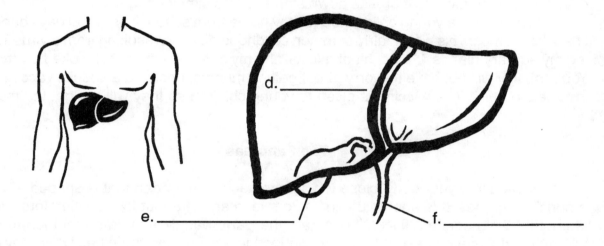

d. _____

e. _____   f. _____

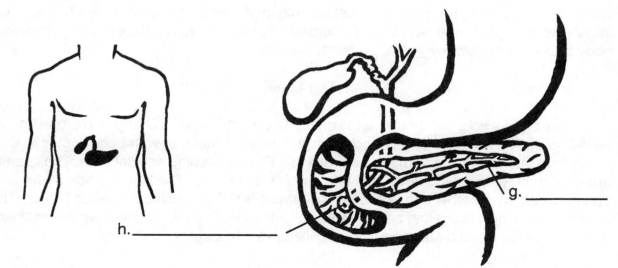

g. _____

h. _____

A Graphic Organizer: The Digestive System

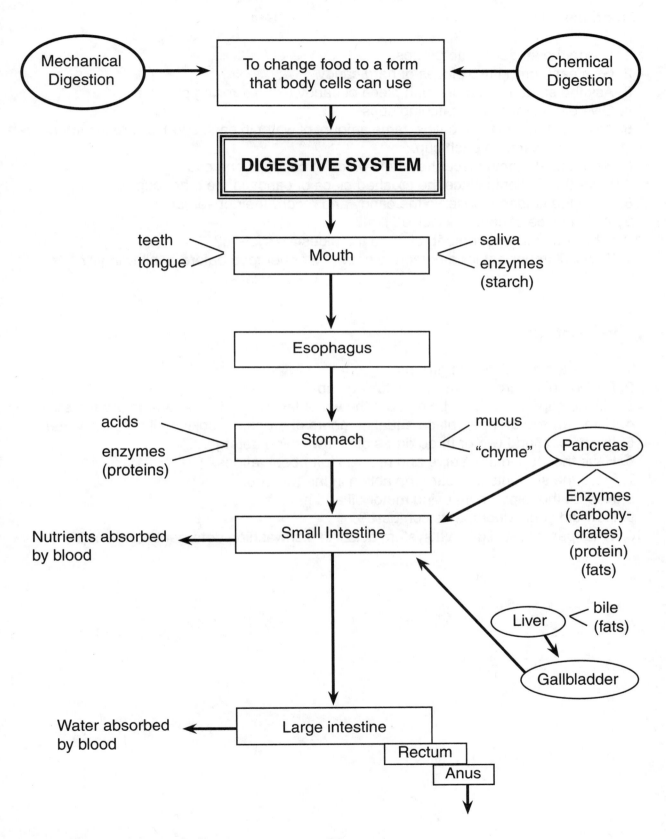

Activities for the Digestive System

Experiment #1:

1. Divide the students into groups.
2. Give each group two pieces of hard candy.
3. Ask the students to crush one piece of candy using a rolling pin.
4. Give each group two matching cups.
5. Ask the students to place the same amount of water in each cup. Be sure the temperature is the same in each cup.
6. Have the students place the whole piece of candy in one cup.
7. Have the students place the crushed piece of candy in the other cup.
8. Have the students observe the candy and record their observations.
9. Which piece of candy dissolved first?
10. Why does this experiment relate to the digestive system?
11. Why is it important for a person to chew his or her food before swallowing it?

Experiment #2:

1. Divide the students into groups.
2. Provide each group with two matching cups.
3. Fill the cups with water, being sure the water levels and temperatures are the same.
4. Using an eye dropper, place equal numbers of drops of cooking oil onto the water.
5. In one cup, add two or three drops of dishwashing detergent.
6. Have the students observe and record their observations.
7. Have the students compare the action in the two cups.
8. Repeat the experiment using motor oil and hand soap.
9. How did your experiments compare?
10. What part of the digestive system acts like dishwashing detergent/hand soap?

Research Activities for the Digestive System

1. Work as a class or assign students to research the following problems associated with the digestive system. Be sure to include a description of the problem, the cause, and the accepted treatment.

Appendicitis
Colic
Constipation
Diarrhea
Flatulence
Gallstones
Heartburn
Indigestion
Jaundice
Obesity
Trichinosis
Ulcers

2. There has been a lot of discussion in recent years regarding eating disorders. Ask students to develop a research file for each of the following disorders. Include newspaper and magazine articles in your file. Ask local health officials to present information to the class.

Anorexia Nervosa
Bulimia

3. Students might consider a career as a dietician. Research the responsiblities of a dietician for each of the following job locations.

A nursing home
A hospital
A weight-loss center
A school
A fitness center
A correctional center

4. In the 1820's William Beaumont performed experiments related to the digestive system. Research his experiments and present his findings to the class.

5. Research the American Dietetic Association. When was it founded? What is its purpose? Who are its members?

Like a Breath of Fresh Air: The Respiratory System

Well, now it is time to discover yet another system in our wonderful machines. This time we will learn about the respiratory system. We will learn how the respiratory system helps our bodies, and we will discover what all the parts of the system are.

People can survive for a week or more without food. It would not be much fun, and we would become very weak, but we could stay alive for a while. People can survive for a few days without water. Do you know how long people can live without oxygen? You can only stay alive for a few minutes if your body does not have oxygen. Why can you live so long without food or water, and die so quickly if you do not have oxygen?

Your body has storage systems for food. When you eat, the nutrients that are not used right away are stored. Those nutrients can then be used in the future when new nutrients are not available. In a similar way, your body is able to store some water. If you do not have a supply of fresh water, you can use the stored water from your body to keep yourself alive. Your body does not, however, have any way to store oxygen. You must provide your body with new oxygen all the time. If you do not have a supply of fresh oxygen, you cannot stay alive.

This is not unique to humans. All organisms exchange gases with their environment. The gases needed and the wastes produced may be different from one organism to another, but all living things must absorb gases from the environment and release waste gases back into the environment.

The respiratory system is responsible for providing your body with the oxygen that it needs. The first job of this system is **to pass oxygen from the air to the blood**. Remember that one of the jobs of the circulatory system is to carry oxygen to all the body cells. The respiratory system brings in the oxygen, and then the circulatory system gets the oxygen to the places where it is needed.

Your circulatory system also removes wastes from your body cells. In order for you to be healthy, your body must have a way to get rid of its wastes. Some of those wastes are gases. They cannot stay in your body. Those wastes leave your cells and enter your blood. The blood carries the gaseous wastes to your respiratory system. The respiratory system then removes them from your body. This is the second job of the respiratory system: **to remove gaseous wastes from the body**.

Now you know why you have to have a respiratory system. Next we will take a look at some of the organs that help your respiratory system do its jobs.

Name: _____ Date: _____

Questions

1. How long can people live without food? Why?

_____

_____

2. How long can people survive without water? Why?

_____

_____

3. Why can't people survive more than a few minutes without oxygen?

_____

4. What do people have in common with all living organisms?

_____

5. What are the two jobs of the respiratory system?

_____

_____

6. Why does the respiratory system need to pass oxygen to the blood?

_____

7. How does the circulatory system help the respiratory system get rid of gaseous wastes?

_____

_____

8. When astronauts travel in space, they must wear special helmets. Why?

_____

9. How are people like trees?

_____

_____

10. Fish are able to breathe underwater. Why can't humans?

_____

_____

Who "Nose" What the Parts of This System Are?

Think about standing in the kitchen. A loaf of bread is in the oven. It smells great. You close your eyes and take a deep breath. Mmm, you can hardly wait until the bread is done and you can eat a piece of it.

The Nose

When you smell the bread, you use your nose. You also use your nose for breathing. That is one of the ways you get oxygen into your body. (Sometimes you breathe through your mouth. This is the other way to get oxygen into your body.) Your nose, or your **nasal cavity**, is the first part of your respiratory system.

Let's take a closer look at your nose. Your nose is stuck in the middle of your face. It has two holes that lead into your head. These holes are called the **nostrils**. Inside your nostrils you have lots of tiny blood vessels. They are very close to the surface. You also have some tiny hairs that are called **cilia**. Finally, you have a moist, sticky fluid in your nose, called mucus.

Why does your nose need to have blood vessels, mucus, and cilia? They each have very important jobs to do. Remember you are bringing air from the environment into your body. Sometimes that air is dirty or the air may carry some kind of disease. You do not want the dirt or disease to get inside your body and spread to other parts of the body. The mucus and cilia are your first protectors. They have the task of making sure the air that goes into the rest of your body is as clean as possible. The sticky mucus traps some of the dust and dirt. The cilia trap more dust and dirt. They also move the dirt and dust out of your respiratory system, in a sneeze or a cough.

Sometimes the air that you are breathing is very cold. The inside of your body is nice and warm, so the air going into it needs to be as warm as possible. The blood vessels inside your nose are very close to the surface, and they are very small. The warm blood moving inside the blood vessels helps heat up the air that you are breathing.

The three jobs of the cilia, mucus, and blood vessels are to moisten, to warm, and to filter the air that you breathe.

The Pharynx

The next part of your respiratory system is called the **pharynx**. Another name for this is the throat. It is a muscular tube that is about five inches long. The pharynx connects the nasal cavity with the trachea. The pharynx is lined with cilia that trap any dirt that may have gotten past the filtering system in the nasal cavity.

The Trachea

The third part of your respiratory system is called the **trachea**. A more common name is the windpipe. As the common name suggests, this is a pipe or tube. It is about 12 inches long. Since you need oxygen all the time, this tube needs to remain open. The trachea is made of smooth muscle (remember that this is involuntary muscle) and is held open by rings of cartilage. The cartilage rings are "C" shaped and most people have between 16 and 20 of them.

If you tilt your head back and gently run your fingers over the outside of your throat, you should be able to feel the cartilage rings in your trachea. Now, if you hold your head up straight, you can gently move the trachea from side to side. You should still be able to feel the cartilage.

The Larynx

At the top of your trachea, you have a very important structure. The **larynx**, or voice box, is a series of folds of tissue surrounded by protective cartilage. When air passes over the folds of tissue, or **vocal cords**, sounds are made. You learn to control the amount of air passing through your larynx. If you want to talk in just a whisper, you need to use just a bit of air. If you want to yell loud enough to be heard across the school yard, you have to use a lot of air. That's why you seem to be out of breath after you have been screaming for a while.

The Epiglottis

When we talked about the digestive system, we said that you have a tube right next to your trachea that is called the esophagus. This tube carries food from your mouth to your stomach. It lies flat when you are not using it and opens up when you swallow. The trachea needs to remain open all the time so air can move from your nasal cavity to your lungs. With the two tubes being so close to each other, you might think it would be easy for food to get headed down the wrong tube.

Your body has a wonderful way of protecting you. At the end of the pharynx, which is also the beginning of the trachea, you have a flap of muscle called the **epiglottis**. When you are breathing, the epiglottis stays out of the way, letting air flow freely into your open trachea. When you swallow, the epiglottis moves to cover your larynx and the opening to your trachea. When the epiglottis moves, it opens up the way for food to move down the esophagus to your stomach. As soon as you have finished swallowing, the epiglottis moves back out of the way, and you are ready to breathe freely.

The Bronchi

At the base of your trachea, your respiratory system splits into two parts. Each part is a tube, called a bronchus. The **bronchi** (plural for bronchus), which lead into the right and left lungs, are made of involuntary muscle and they have rings of cartilage, similar to the trachea. The bronchi, however, are smaller. These tubes continue to clean and moisten the air that you breathe in with the mucus that lines them.

The Bronchioles and Alveoli

In the lungs, the bronchi become smaller and smaller. These tiny tubes are called **bronchioles**. The smallest bronchioles are surrounded by tiny clusters of air sacs. They almost look like bunches of grapes surrounding tiny branches on an upside down tree! The air sacs are called **alveoli**. Scientists believe there are about 300 million alveoli in each lung! The air sacs are able to expand and contract. When they are filled with air, they resemble tiny balloons. When the air is exhaled out of your lungs, the air sacs deflate like empty balloons, ready to take in new air with the next breath.

Each alveolus (singular for alveoli) in your lungs is surrounded by tiny blood vessels. Oxygen brought into your lungs through the respiratory system is able to pass through the walls of the alveolus and into the blood capillary. In a similar way, waste gases carried to the lungs by the circulatory system are able to pass from the capillaries to the alveoli so they can be removed from the body.

More About Your Lungs

Together, the bronchioles and the alveoli make up your **lungs**. Your two lungs are cone-shaped organs made of spongy tissue. They are elastic in nature, being able to stretch larger when you inhale and return to smaller size when you exhale. The left lung is slightly smaller than the right lung because it needs to leave extra room for the tip of the heart!

If you were to spread a pair of lungs out flat, they would cover a huge area. If you were to spread out the entire skin of an average human, the lungs would be more than 20 times bigger than the skin. Remember, you must have oxygen to stay alive. It is needed by all the cells in your body and you do not have any way to store oxygen for later use. The large surface area of your lungs allows you to absorb a great deal of oxygen each time you breathe.

The Diaphragm

The final part of your respiratory system is a large sheet of muscle called the **diaphragm**. This muscle separates your chest from the lower part of your body. The diaphragm lies just under your ribs and looks like a small dome. When you inhale, the diaphragm contracts and moves down. When you exhale, the diaphragm relaxes and moves back up to its resting position.

Wow, that's a lot of information to learn. Try to remember that the respiratory system beins with the nasal cavity. Air leaving the nasal cavity travels through the pharynx, trachea, larynx, bronchi, bronchioles, and alveoli. The oxygen then moves into the blood and the first job of the respiratory system is done. Waste gases move from the blood into the alveoli. The wastes then travel through the bronchioles, bronchi, trachea, larynx, pharynx and leave your body through your mouth or nose. That completes the second job of the respiratory system.

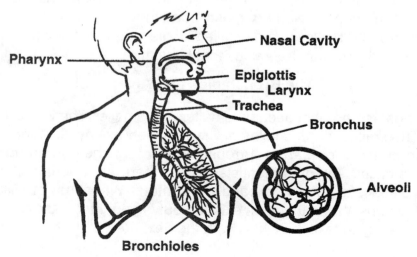

Name: _____ Date: _____

Questions

1. What is the more common name for each of these parts of the respiratory system?
   a. Alveoli _____   b. Nasal Cavity _____
   c. Cilia _____   d. Pharynx _____
   e. Larynx _____   f. Trachea _____

2. What are the three jobs done by the blood vessels, cilia, and mucus in your nasal cavity?

   _____

   _____

3. Why is it better to breathe in through your nose instead of breathing in through your mouth?

   _____

4. Why does the pharynx need to have cilia?

   _____

5. Why does your trachea need to have cartilage rings?

   _____

6. Suppose you want to whisper to the student next to you in class, what must you remember to do with your vocal cords?

   _____

7. Why do you need two bronchi?

   _____

8. What do the lungs look like? (You may draw a picture.)

9. How can the oxygen you bring into your body get into the circulatory system?

   _____

10. What position must the diaphragm be in when you inhale? When you exhale?

   _____

   _____

What Is Breathing?

Breathing is something you do all day long, every day, from the moment you are born until you reach the end of your life. You breathe without really thinking about it. It is an involuntary action. Let's take a close look at what is going on inside your body when you breathe.

Inspiration

The first part of the process of breathing is called **inspiration**. It involves the taking in of oxygen through the parts of the respiratory system. Why does air move from your environment into your lungs? Let's take a look.

First, the diaphragm contracts. Remember, when this large sheet of muscle contracts, it moves down. At the same time, the muscles in the chest contract. These muscles pull the ribs up and out. The **sternum**, or breast bone, is also raised. As a result of the movement of the diaphragm, chest muscles, ribs, and sternum, the chest cavity becomes larger. When the size of the chest cavity changes, the air pressure in the chest changes also. There is more room in the chest for the air that is there, so there is less air pressure.

Air naturally moves from an area with higher air pressure, to an area with lower air pressure. When the chest cavity has lower air pressure, air from outside the body moves in, trying to equalize the pressure. This is when you inhale.

Expiration

The second part of the process of breathing is called **expiration**. This involves the removal of waste gases from the respiratory system. Why does air move out of your lungs back into the environment? Let's take a look at this part of the process now.

First, the diaphragm relaxes. This means the large sheet of muscle will move back up to its starting position under the ribs. At the same time, the chest muscles relax, letting the ribs fall back down and in. The sternum also falls back to its original position. This time when the diaphragm, chest muscles, ribs, and sternum all move, the cavity becomes smaller. The air pressure inside the chest cavity changes again. This time there is less room for the air that there is, so the air pressure increases.

Once again, air moves from an area with higher pressure to an area with lower pressure. When the chest cavity has a higher air pressure, some of the air moves out of the body. A new pressure balance is attained when you exhale.

The Air You Breathe

When you take a deep breath, you inhale air into your body. Just what does that air consist of? When you let out a deep breath, you exhale air out of your body. Just what does that air consist of? Take a good look at the following charts.

Inhaled Air	Exhaled Air
20.9% Oxygen	16.3% Oxygen
79.0% Nitrogen	79.0% Nitrogen
0.07% Carbon Dioxide	4.50% Carbon Dioxide
0.03% Other Gases	0.20% Other Gases

Name: _____ Date: _____

Questions

1. What is inspiration?

_____

2. What is expiration?

_____

3. Which body parts are responsible for making the chest cavity larger when you inhale?

_____

_____

4. Which body parts are responsible for making the chest cavity smaller when you exhale?

_____

_____

5. What happens to the air pressure in your chest cavity when your diaphragm contracts?

_____

6. What happens to the air pressure in your chest cavity when your diaphragm relaxes?

_____

7. Why does air move in or out of your respiratory system?

_____

_____

8. How much oxygen do you inhale? Exhale?

_____

_____

9. Why does the amount of oxygen change?

_____

_____

10. Why is the percentage of nitrogen inhaled and exhaled the same?

_____

_____

Respiration: What Is It?

We have been learning about the respiratory system: it's jobs and parts. We have even looked closely at the process of breathing. Now we need to try to understand what respiration is. After all, the system seems to have been named for it!

Respiration is a process that takes place in your body cells. Sometimes it is called internal respiration or cellular respiration. It is the process by which oxygen actually combines with glucose to release energy. Let's take a look at the sequence leading to respiration, step by step.

First, we need to refresh our memories a bit. Remember when we learned about the digestive system? We said the job of that system was to change the food we eat to a form that body cells can use. When food passes through the digestive system, it is broken down into simple molecules. One type of molecule that your body cells must have is called **glucose**. Glucose moves from the digestive system into the circulatory system. The circulatory system then carries the glucose to each of the body cells.

Okay, now we can go back to the respiratory system. We know that breathing brings oxygen into the body. The oxygen passes from the air through the respiratory system and ends up in the alveoli in the lungs.

The circulatory system plays the next part in the sequence. Tiny capillaries surround the alveoli. The oxygen molecules pass from the lungs into the blood. The circulatory system then delivers the oxygen to the body cells.

When the oxygen arrives in the body cells, it combines with the glucose provided by the digestive and circulatory systems. When the glucose and oxygen combine in a chemical reaction, energy is released. Wastes are also produced. The wastes are carbon dioxide and water. The combination of the two materials, the release of energy, and the production of the waste materials is the process known as respiration.

The circulatory system plays a second role in this sequence. The carbon dioxide produced during respiration must be removed from the cells. It moves into the capillaries and is carried through the circulatory system until it arrives at the lungs. There, the tiny capillaries surrounding the alveoli surrender the waste gas to the respiratory system.

After the molecules of carbon dioxide have moved into the lungs, expiration occurs. By breathing, the waste gases are exhaled from the body, and the entire sequence is ready to begin again.

The Sequence for Respiration

Breathing — Oxygen is inhaled.
Circulation — Oxygen is carried to cells.
Respiration — Oxygen and glucose combine in a chemical reaction to release energy.
Circulation — Carbon dioxide is carried to the lungs.
Breathing — Carbon dioxide is exhaled.

The Chemical Equation of Respiration

$$C_6H_{12}O_6 + 6O_2 \longrightarrow (energy) \text{ and } 6CO_2 + 6H_2O$$

Name: _____ Date: _____

Questions

1. Where does respiration take place?

_____

2. How does the digestive system work with the respiratory system in the sequence for respiration?

_____

_____

3. How does the circulatory system work with the respiratory system in the sequence for respiration?

_____

_____

4. What two things must combine during respiration?

_____

5. What does respiration release?

_____

6. What are the wastes created during respiration?

_____

7. What is the chemical equation for respiration?

_____

8. Look at the boxes below. Using the words from the word bank, fill in the boxes in the correct sequence for respiration. Some words will be used more than once.
   WORD BANK: **breathing   circulation   respiration**

   [ ]—[ ]—[ ]—[ ]—[ ]

9. When I have a cold, it is hard for me to breathe. I don't have much energy. Why do you think this happens? (Consider the process of respiration.)

_____

_____

10. My mother has always told me it is important to go outside every day and get some fresh air. Was she correct?

_____

A Graphic Organizer:
The Respiratory System

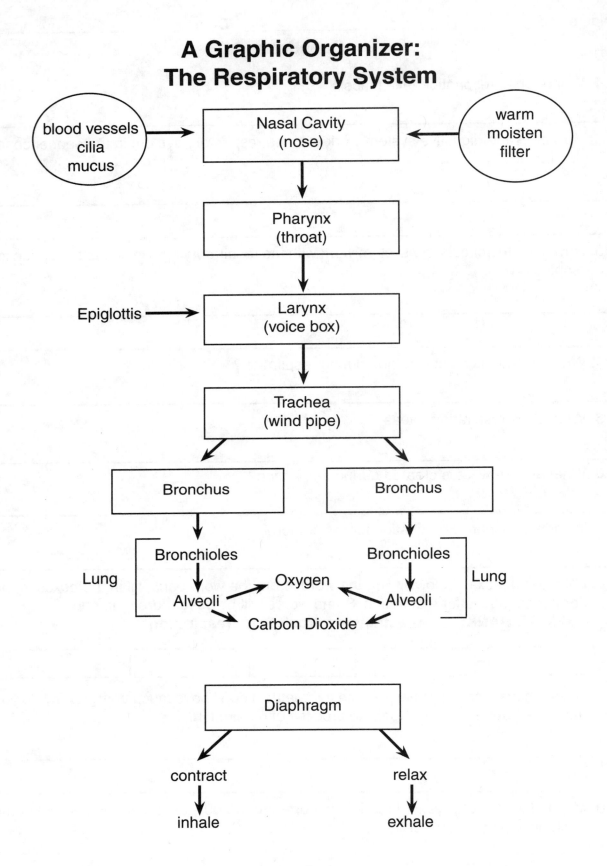

Activities for the Respiratory System

Activity #1:

To demonstrate how air moves from an area of greater pressure to an area of lower pressure, use an "empty" plastic bottle. Discuss with the students the fact that the bottle is not actually empty but contains air. The air pressure inside and outside of the bottle are equal.

Press the sides of the bottle together. Have the students feel the flow of air leaving the bottle. Explain that pushing the sides closer together created less space inside the bottle, which meant the air was under greater pressure. The air moved out of the bottle in an attempt to equalize the pressure again. Ask the students what they think will happen when you let go of the sides of the bottle.

Let go of the bottle and have the students notice that air returns to the inside of the container. By letting go of the sides, you have increased the amount of space inside the bottle and decreased the air pressure. Air from the environment enters the bottle to equalize the air pressure.

Repeat the experiment. This time explain how the activity resembles movement of air in and out of the lungs.

Activity #2:

Have students measure their resting breathing rates. Ask the students to count the number of times they exhale in 15 seconds. Have them multiply that number by four. (You may have them count for 30 seconds and multiply by two or do a full minute of counting without any multiplying.) Record the results and repeat the procedure two more times. Find an average for the three trials. Record the average.

Ask the students to run in place for two minutes, then ask them to count the number of times they exhale again. Be sure you count and multiply the same way you did in the first part of the activity. Record the results and repeat the procedure two more times. Once again, find the average and record your results.

Compare the results for the resting breathing rate and the exercising breathing rate. You may expand this experiment by recording the results after a number of different activities such as singing, jumping, running races, and so on.

Activity #3:

Obtain some lime water, test tubes, and clean straws. Pour a small amount of lime water in each test tube. Be sure you have measured carefully and used the same amount in each tube.

Have students exhale GENTLY through the straw into the lime water. Students should continue for two minutes. Be sure the students observe each other's test tubes during this time. At the end of two minutes, ask students to record their observations. Save one test tube. Pour the same amount of lime water into an empty test tube, but do not have any students exhale into this water. This will serve as a control.

What happened to the lime water? What caused the lime water to change color? What waste gas made the lime water change color?

Research Ideas for the Respiratory System

1. Divide the students into groups. Have each group pick one of the following disorders of the respiratory system. Each group should prepare a written or oral report including the symptoms, causes, and treatments for each ailment.

   upper respiratory infection   otitis
   sinusitis   pneumonia
   tonsillitis   emphysema
   hoarseness   bronchitis
   pleurisy   asthma
   lung cancer   tuberculosis
   tumors   hiccups

2. As a class, research the proper techniques for performing the Hiemlich maneuver and CPR. If possible, have someone demonstrate the procedures for the class. Emphasize the importance of proper training.

3. Ask a professional singer to visit your class. Discuss the type of training that must be done to maintain the proper stamina. Discuss the need to exercise the diaphragm, chest, throat, mouth, and jaw muscles. If possible, have the class learn some of the breathing exercises and warm up routines used before a performance.

4. Discuss how mountain climbing affects the respiratory system. Research the type of equipment needed for high-altitude climbing. Explore some of the negative side effects that can be experienced.

5. Discuss SCUBA diving. Research the origin of the word *scuba* as well as the equipment that must be used. Have students list the training needed as well as famous scuba diving locations around the world.

It All Goes Up In Smoke
Tobacco and the Respiratory System

1. Smoking has become a hot topic in today's society. There is a lot of concern about the number of young people who smoke. In an effort to help the students in your class make the most informed decision possible, research the following topics.

   Native Americans and their use of tobacco
   Commercially grown tobacco (beginning in 1612)
   The invention of cigarette-making machines (1880s)

2. There are a number of laws now in effect that restrict the use of tobacco. Research the tobacco laws in effect in your state and community. Research federal restrictions as well. Some areas to consider are:

   age restrictions;
   smoking in public transportation, especially planes;
   smoking in restaurants;
   smoking in public buildings and on school grounds.

3. Another "hot topic" relates to advertising. Discuss why the tobacco industry is interested in advertising. Also discuss the restrictions placed on tobacco products: the use of TV and radio, the placement of tobacco ads in public places such as ball parks, and the kinds of ads that are being used.

   Plan a debate. Divide the students into two teams. Ask one team to support the advertisement of tobacco under freedom of speech. Ask the other team to condemn the advertisement of tobacco as a public health and safety issue.

   Ask students to develop two lists. The first should include the reasons why people might want to smoke. The second list would include reasons why people would not smoke. Compare the lists, and discuss.

4. Passive smoking or second-hand smoke is a concern for many people. Ask a local health official to discuss the effects of passive smoking. Discuss ways that students might avoid becoming second-hand smokers.

You Can't Keep It All: The Excretory System

So far you have learned about five of the systems in the machine that is your body. You have discovered that the systems have special jobs to do and they have many parts to help them do their jobs. Now it is time to learn about the next system: the excretory system. We will explore its job and its parts.

Getting Rid of Wastes

The excretory system has one main job, and it is a very important one. It must remove wastes from the body. Your body actually makes three different kinds of wastes: solid, liquid, and gaseous. Each kind of waste is removed by a different part of your body. Let's see how that is done.

Working Together to Get the Job Done

There are four main parts that work together to remove all the wastes from the body. You have already learned about two of them. First of all, **solid food wastes** are removed by the **large intestine**. You should remember that the large intestine is part of the digestive system. When the nutrients and water have been removed from your food, the remaining wastes are stored in the end of the large intestines. Remember this area is called the **rectum**. The wastes are actually removed from the body through the **anus**. The large intestine takes care of the solid wastes.

The second part of the body that removes wastes is the **lungs**. When you studied the respiratory system, you learned that the **alveoli** in the lungs allow oxygen to move into the blood and also accept waste gases from the blood. The waste gases are passed from the lungs to the atmosphere. The lungs take care of the **gaseous wastes** in your body.

That leaves us with the **liquid wastes**. They are removed by the **urinary system** and by the **skin**. We need to take a closer look at these parts of the body so we can fully understand just how liquid wastes are removed.

Name: _____ Date: _____

Questions and Review

Match the following systems with their jobs.

S = Skeletal   M = Muscular   C = Circulatory
D = Digestive   R = Respiratory   E = Excretory

1. _____ to carry food, water, and oxygen to the body cells

2. _____ to protect body organs

3. _____ to pass oxygen from the air to the blood

4. _____ to remove wastes from the body cells

5. _____ to change food to a form that the body cells can use

6. _____ to give the body its basic shape

7. _____ to help with movement

8. _____ to remove solid, liquid, and gaseous wastes from the body

9. _____ to remove gaseous wastes from the body

10. _____ to give the body its final shape

11. Which organ in your body removes solid food wastes?

_____

12. Which organ in your body removes gaseous wastes?

_____

13. What are two ways that liquid wastes are removed from your body?

_____

_____

The Urinary System

The urinary system is responsible for removing most of the liquid wastes from your body. The urinary system can be divided into four important parts: the kidneys, the ureters, the bladder, and the urethra.

The Kidneys

Normally, you have two **kidneys**. They are shaped like lima beans and are found just above your waist, near your spine, on the back of your body. Each kidney is about 10 centimeters long and about five centimeters wide in an adult. The kidneys are just a bit larger in men than they are in women. Kidneys are surrounded by layers of fat. This fat supports the kidneys, helping them stay in the right place, and it protects them, too.

Arteries carry your blood through your body. When your blood arrives at a kidney, it moves from the arteries into capillaries. Some of the substances in the blood are too large to move into the tiny capillaries, so those substances stay in the arteries, ready to move on to other parts of the body. Blood cells and protein molecules are two good examples. The other substances, such as water, salts, and some nutrients are small enough to fit into the capillaries in the kidneys.

Inside each kidney, you have about a million tiny filtering units called **nephrons**. The nephrons have the responsibility of cleaning your blood. The capillaries in your kidneys carry your blood into the nephrons. As the blood travels through the nephrons, food molecules, salts, urea, and water are forced into special collecting tubes. The food molecules, most of the water, and some of the salts are able to return to the blood stream. They travel from the capillaries into veins and continue their journey through the body. The rest of the water, salts, and urea stay in the collection tubes. These substances become **urine**.

Your kidneys clean all of the blood in your body more than 50 times each day. For most people, the urinary system only makes about one or 1.5 liters of urine in a day's time. Urine is about 95 percent water. The other five percent is urea, acids, and salts.

The Ureters

Normally, you have two tubes that are connected to your kidneys. They are called **ureters**. The ureters are very narrow tubes that may be 10 to 12 inches long. They move urine from the kidneys to the next part of the urinary system, the bladder.

Bladder

The **bladder** is a muscular sac. It can stretch and then return to its original size. When urine leaves the kidneys, it travels through the ureters and arrives in the bladder. As more and more urine arrives during the day, your bladder gets larger and larger. Your bladder should be able to hold about one liter of urine. When your bladder feels full, special muscles at the bottom of the bladder help you release the urine.

The Urethra

When urine is released from the bladder, it travels into the **urethra**. The urethra is a tube that leads from the bladder out of the body. It is the last part of the urinary system.

The Urinary Tract

All together, the kidneys, ureters, bladder and urethra are called the **urinary tract**. This very important system is responsible for making sure that wastes do not build up inside your body.

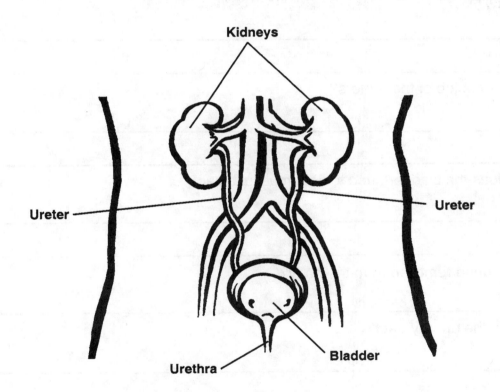

Kidneys

Ureter

Ureter

Urethra

Bladder

Name: _____ Date: _____

Questions

1. What are the four important parts of the urinary system?

_____

_____

2. What is the main job of the kidneys?

_____

3. Which part of the kidneys serve as a filter?

_____

4. What happens if you drink a lot of extra water?

_____

_____

5. What is the job of the ureters?

_____

_____

6. Why does the bladder need to be a muscular sac?

_____

_____

7. How is urine removed from the body?

_____

8. What is the urinary tract?

_____

_____

9. Sometimes your body makes a lot of urine in one day. Other times, your body makes less urine. Why?

_____

_____

10. Why do infants and toddlers need to use diapers?

_____

What a Waste!

Do you remember visiting the doctor's office? Maybe a nurse gave you a small cup and asked you to go to the bathroom. The nurse wanted you to bring back some urine. Sometimes that can be a bit embarassing. Did you ever wonder why you had to do that?

Urine is a waste, but it can be used to learn many things about your health. After the nurse gets the urine sample from you, different tests can be done. If your urine is clear and does not have any bacteria in it, it probably means you are in good health. If your urine has some sugar in it, you might have a disease called diabetes. If your urine has protein in it, you might have a problem with your kidneys. If your urine has blood in it, you might have injured parts of your urinary system somehow. Maybe you even have a urinary tract infection.

The doctor wants to know if you are having problems like diabetes, kidney problems, or urinary tract infections. The doctor cannot see the parts inside your body, so the tests are a good way to understand what is happening inside of you. Your nurse and doctor are really not trying to embarrass you, they are only trying to make sure that you are as healthy as you can be.

Kidney Failure

Sometimes a kidney stops working. Maybe it stopped because of an accident or because of an illness. Most of the time, the other kidney takes over and does the work that would normally be done by the two kidneys. People have lived for many years, and been very healthy, with only one working kidney.

If both kidneys stop working, it is a more serious problem. A special machine might be needed to clean your blood. A dialysis machine uses a tube to connect to the body's arteries. The blood travels through the machine and is filtered by the machine instead of being filtered by the nephrons in the kidneys. The clean blood is returned to the body. Dialysis may need to be done two or three times a week and can take several hours each time.

Instead of using a dialysis machine, some people have kidney transplants. During a kidney transplant operation, the patient receives a healthy kidney from another person. Hopefully, the person's body will accept the new kidney, and it will work for many years to clean that person's blood.

Name: _____ Date: _____

Questions

1. Why does a doctor or nurse want a urine sample from each patient?

_____

_____

2. What does it mean if your urine is clear, without bacteria?

_____

3. What does it mean if your urine contains sugar?

_____

4. What does it mean if your urine contains protein?

_____

5. What does it mean if your urine contains blood?

_____

_____

6. How many kidneys do most healthy people have?

_____

7. What can happen if one kidney stops working?

_____

8. What happens if both kidneys stop working?

_____

_____

9. What happens in a kidney transplant?

_____

_____

10. If Sue needs a new kidney, who would probably be the best kidney donor?
    a. her best friend
    b. her husband
    c. her sister
    d. a neighbor
    Why?_____

_____

Name: _____ Date: _____

That's No Sweat!

Imagine that you are riding your bicycle. It is summer, and it is hot! The sun is beating down on you, and there is no breeze in the air. You have on a dark shirt and pants. How does your skin feel? What about your hair?

You are probably imagining that you are sweating. Your body is doing two things when you are sweating. First, your body is trying to find a way to cool you off. It is not good for too much heat to build up inside your body. When you sweat, liquid appears on your skin. (We call it sweat.) Some of the heat from your body is used to evaporate that liquid. When the heat energy is used for evaporation, your body begins to cool itself down a little bit. You sweat to control your body temperature.

You also sweat to get rid of body wastes. Your skin has sweat glands in it. When blood arrives at the sweat glands, some of the water, urea, and salts are removed from the blood. Your sweat is mostly water, but it also has urea and salts in it. The sweat moves from the glands through holes in your skin that are called **pores**. When the water in the sweat evaporates to cool off your body, the urea and salts stay on your skin. They will stay there until you wash them off.

Questions

1. How is your skin like the urinary system?

_____

_____

2. How is your skin like a thermometer?

_____

_____

3. Sometimes when I am working very hard in my garden, a drop of sweat will roll down my face and end up in the corner of my mouth. Why does that sweat taste salty?

_____

_____

4. Why is it important to take a bath or shower after you have been sweating?

_____

_____

5. Why do people sweat more in the hot summers than they do in the cool winters?

_____

_____

A Graphic Organizer:
The Excretory System

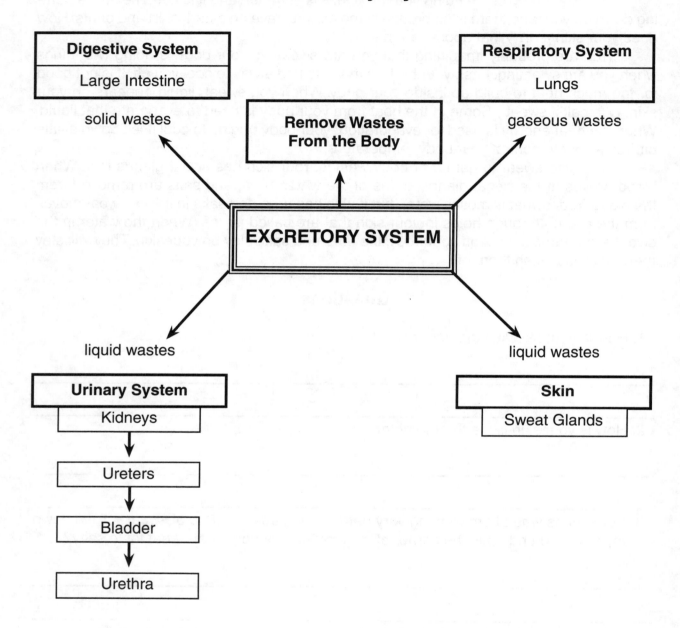

Digestive System
Large Intestine

solid wastes

Remove Wastes From the Body

Respiratory System
Lungs

gaseous wastes

EXCRETORY SYSTEM

liquid wastes

liquid wastes

Urinary System
Kidneys

Ureters

Bladder

Urethra

Skin
Sweat Glands

Activities for the Excretory System

Activity #1:

This activity will demonstrate the removal of water through the skin.

Materials: Plastic Bags
               Rubber Bands
               Stop Watch

Procedure: 1. Have students observe the plastic bags.
               2. Record the observations
               3. Have each student place a plastic bag over one hand.
                  Secure the bags with a rubber band around the wrist.
               4. Leave the bags on their hands for five minutes.
               5. Have students observe any changes in the bag.
               6. Record the observations.
               7. Remove the bags and dispose of them properly.

(*Remind students not to do experiments of any kind without adult supervision.*)

Activity #2:

This activity will demonstrate that some water is removed by the respiratory system.

Materials: Small Hand Mirrors

Procedure: 1. Ask students to observe the hand mirrors.
               2. Record the observations.
               3. Ask each student to hold the mirror close to his/her mouth.
               4. Have the students observe the mirror.
               5. Record the observations.
               6. Steps 3–5 can be repeated several times.

Research Ideas for the Excretory System

Hopefully, your students have never experienced the pain associated with kidney stones. They may, however, know someone who has had them. It may be helpful to have your students research kidney stones. They should try to determine what causes the stones, what the symptoms are, and what kinds of treatment are available.

Urinary tract infections are not infrequent in school-aged children. Invite the school nurse, a local doctor, or someone from the local health department to speak to the students. The causes, symptoms, and most common remedies should be discussed. Students may not be comfortable asking specific questions in front of their peers. You may wish to provide a question box for the students a day or two ahead of your speaker's arrival. As the teacher, you can pose the questions in a professional, non-embarrassing manner.

Keeping It All Going: The Nervous System

You have learned a lot about your wonderful machine. You should have a much better understanding of what the parts are and how they do their jobs. You should be getting the idea that the different parts of your body need to work together so it can be the best working machine possible. Now, we need to see what keeps all the parts and systems working together. We need to look at the nervous system and learn about its jobs and parts.

Coordinating the Body Systems

Your nervous system has a big job to do. It must make sure that all the different systems in the body work together. The nervous system can never rest. It has to make sure your circulatory system is working and keeping your heart beating. At the same time, it has to make sure your respiratory system is keeping you breathing. It has to control all of your movements, your learning, your feelings, and so on.

When all the systems are working correctly, your body is in balance. This balance is called **homeostasis**. The nervous system has the tremendous job of keeping the proper homeostasis in your body.

Five More Jobs

The nervous system has five more jobs to do at the same time. Your nervous system is responsible for maintaining your consciousness. You need to be alert and aware of the things happening around you. You need to be able to respond to those things. Your nervous system helps you do that.

Another job of the nervous system is to coordinate what you sense or feel. Your ears, eyes, nose, skin, and tongue are all organs that allow you to sense things. Your nervous system helps you understand what you are sensing or feeling. It also helps you know what to do about those feelings.

When you were little, there were a lot of things you did not know. You started experiencing things and learning. Your nervous system was responsible for your consciousness, your senses, your reactions to your senses, as well as your learning and your memory. It is a good idea to take good care of your nervous system since it does so much work to take care of you!

Dividing Things Up

The nervous system is divided into two parts. The first part is called the **central nervous system**. It is made up of the brain and the spinal cord. These two parts of your body keep you alive. It is very important to keep them safe and protected. (Remember, that is one of the jobs of the skeletal system.) Your brain is protected by your skull, and your spinal cord is protected by the vertebrae in your spine.

The rest of your nervous system is called the **peripheral nervous system**. The word *peripheral* means "outside." The peripheral nervous system is all the other nerves in your body including 12 pairs of cranial nerves coming from your head and 31 pairs of spinal nerves coming from your backbone.

When you studied the muscular system, you learned that you can control some muscles, the voluntary ones. Involuntary muscles, like your cardiac and your smooth muscles, are not controlled by you. Do you know what controls those muscles? Of course, it is the nervous system. You might hear people talk about the **autonomic nervous system**. Those are the nerves that are responsible for your involuntary muscles.

Your nervous system works hard to control the parts of your body. The nervous system is responsible for immediate responses to the environment. Most of the effects of the nervous system are quick and last a short time. Without a properly functioning nervous system, you cannot have a properly functioning body.

Name: _____ Date: _____

Questions

1. What is the main job of the nervous system?

_____

_____

2. When a person is unconscious, which body system is responsible for that condition?

_____

3. What are your five senses?

_____

_____

4. Why is your nervous system important to you when you are in school?

_____

_____

5. Which part of the nervous system is the brain and spinal cord?

_____

6. How does the skeletal system help the nervous system?

_____

_____

7. Which part of the nervous system do the nerves in your arms and legs belong to? Why?

_____

_____

8. How does the nervous system react to the environment?

_____

_____

_____

Name: _____   Date: _____

Are Nerves Really Made of Steel?

If you are very brave and rarely become nervous, someone might say that you have nerves of steel. Of course, your nerves are not really made of steel. Nerves are parts of the nervous system. They are made of special cells called **neurons**.

Okay, now that you know nerves are made of cells called neurons, you might ask what a neuron looks like. Well, each neuron has a cell body. Coming out of the body are branches, or arms. One kind of arm is called a **dendrite**. Dendrites receive messages and carry them to the **nucleus** in the center of the cell. The other kind of arm is called an **axon**. Axons carry messages away from the center of the cell towards other cells. Messages always travel one way: from a dendrite through the cell body to an axon.

There are three different kinds of neuron cells. The first kind is called a **sensory neuron**. This kind of cell gathers information and sends it to your brain or to your spinal cord. The second kind of neuron is called an **interphase neuron**. This kind of cell receives information from a sensory neuron. It passes the information along to the third kind of neuron, a **motor neuron**. A motor neuron carries the information to muscles or glands in the body.

Let's see if we can figure this out better with an example. Imagine you are outside, riding on your bike. You are going down the street, enjoying the beautiful weather. You see a red stop sign. Your sensory neurons in your eyes gather that information. The sensory neurons carry the information to your brain. In your brain, the information is passed to an interphase neuron. Then the interphase neuron passes the information along to a motor neuron. The motor neuron travels to your leg muscles and tells those muscles to help you stop the bicycle.

Nerves need to be close to each other so they can pass information from one cell to the next. They do not, however, actually touch each other. There is an empty space, called a **synapse**, between neurons. When an axon from one nerve is carrying information to the dendrite of another nerve, it uses special chemicals to send the information. The chemicals travel from the axon through the synapse to the next neuron without actually coming into direct contact with the next neuron.

Activity

Using the information you learned about nerves, label the parts of the neuron in the following diagram.

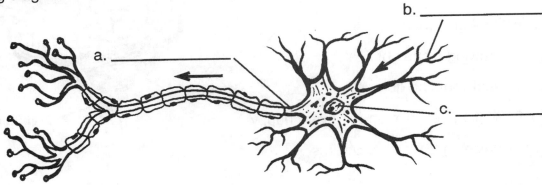

a. _____

b. _____

c. _____

Name: _____ Date: _____

She's a Real Brain!

The main organ of the nervous system is the brain. Scientists have found that the brain can be divided into three parts or areas. They have been able to determine what is controlled by each part of the brain.

The largest part of the brain is called the **cerebrum**. This area of the brain has many folds that increase the total area of the brain. Because this area of the brain is larger, it can have more neurons. The cerebrum controls all conscious body movements. This area of the brain also interprets the information gathered by your senses.

The cerebrum is divided into halves or hemispheres. The left hemisphere controls your ability to speak, use math, and think logically. The right half of the cerebrum controls your musical abilities, your artistic skills, and your emotions. Which side of your cerebrum do you think you use more?

The next part of your brain is called the **cerebellum**. While the cerebrum controls all the voluntary muscles in your body, the cerebellum makes sure your movements are smooth and coordinated. It also controls your balance and your muscle tone.

The last part of your brain is the **brain stem**. This area connects your brain with your spinal cord. Many of your automatic body processes are controlled by the brain stem. It controls your heartbeat, your breathing, and your blood pressure.

Questions

Think about the three main parts of the brain. Which part would you use for each of the following activities?

CBR = cerebrum   CBL = cerebellum   BSM = brain stem

_____ 1. Smelling a fire burning

_____ 2. Running and dribbling a basketball

_____ 3. Breathing

_____ 4. Touching a cold glass

_____ 5. Eating a sour pickle

_____ 6. Seeing a bright light

_____ 7. Drawing a straight line

_____ 8. Heart beating quickly

_____ 9. Smiling because you are very happy

_____ 10. Finishing 20 math problems

Name: _____ Date: _____

Ouch! That's Hot! Reflex Actions

Last week I was working in the kitchen. I cooked some eggs and then started to do the dishes. I forgot to turn off the burner. My daughter came in and started to talk. We were discussing the football game she had seen the night before. I was paying attention to her and forgot about the burner. As she explained about her team's win, I set my hand down on the stove. OUCH! The burner was hot. It burned my finger. Do you know what I did? I pulled my hand away from the hot burner as quickly as I could. It all happened very fast.

Using what you know about the nervous system, let's try to figure out what happened inside my body. First, when my finger touched the hot burner, sensory neurons gathered information about the temperature. Those neurons carried the information to my spinal cord. There was not enough time to send the information all the way to my brain, through the interneurons, then back to my finger through motor neurons. Instead, the information passed from the spinal cord directly to motor neurons. They hurried the information to my arm and finger, and the muscles contracted so I could pull away.

This kind of quick reaction, which does not directly involve the brain, is called a **reflex**. Blinking your eye is another reflex action that happens when you have something too close to your eye. When something gets inside your nose and tickles you, you will sneeze to get it out. That is another reflex action. Has a doctor ever tapped your knee with a small rubber mallet? The doctor was testing your reflexes. Reflex actions are very important for keeping us healthy and safe.

Activity

Develop a graphic organizer showing the path of information when you burn your finger on a hot stove.

A Graphic Organizer: The Nervous System

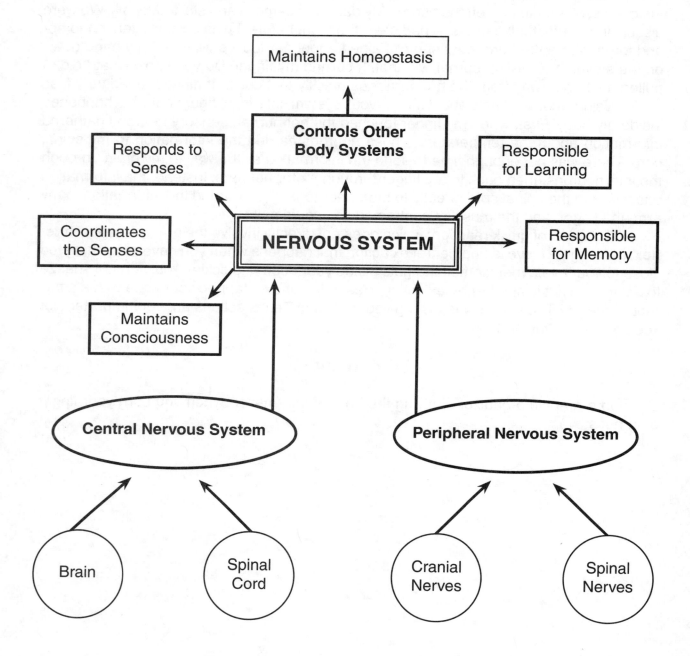

It Takes a Long Time: The Endocrine System

The nervous system does not control your body all by itself. It has some help from another system called the **endocrine system**. The nervous system uses signals sent along nerves to tell other parts of the body what to do. The endocrine system uses chemicals, released into the blood, to tell other systems what to do. The nervous system controls the body quickly, and the results are over with quickly. The endocrine system, however, may take a long time to react, and the effects may last for days, weeks, months, or even years.

The endocrine system uses chemicals, called **hormones**, to control other body systems. The hormones are released into the blood. The circulatory system then carries the chemicals throughout the body. When the chemicals arrive in the right places, at the **target tissues**, they start to do their work. Let's take a look at some of the glands in the endocrine system and see what their hormones can do for your body.

The Thyroid

The **thyroid** is a butterfly-shaped gland found in the throat. The thyroid releases the hormone called **thyroxine**, which controls your body's metabolism. The **metabolism** is all the chemical reactions that happen in your body.

When I was growing up, I was very skinny. I had a high metabolism. My body used up the food I ate very quickly. I could eat and eat, and I never seemed to gain weight. My youngest sister had a slower metabolism. Her body did not use up her food as quickly. When she ate, she gained weight very easily. Later, as I got older, my metabolism started to slow down. I noticed that I started to gain weight. I had to learn to eat less and less because my body was not using up the food as quickly. My sister's metabolism did not slow down as much. She had already learned how to eat less. My metabolism will probably continue to slow down more and more as I get older. I will have to be careful about my eating habits!

The thyroid is not able to work properly if it doesn't have **iodine**. Iodine is an element that is often found in seafood. It may also be added to salt. Look in your cabinet at home. Do you have iodized salt? It is good for your thyroid. If your thyroid does not have enough iodine, it will get larger and larger. An enlarged thyroid is called a **goiter**. They are not very common now because most people use iodized salt on their food.

The Parathyroids

On the back of your thyroid, you have four, small, pea-sized glands called the **parathyroids**. These glands release hormones that help control the amount of phosphate and calcium in your blood. You need to have enough calcium in your body so you can have healthy teeth and bones. It is also important for clotting your blood. Your nerves and muscles use calcium, too. Phosphate helps you to keep the right pH level in your blood. You don't want your blood to have too much acid or to be too alkaline.

If your body makes too much of the parathyroid hormone, however, your bones may become brittle. They will not have the right level of calcium, and they may break easily.

Adrenal Glands

Two very important endocrine glands are found on top of your kidneys. They are called the **adrenal glands**. Each one of these glands has an inner layer and an outer layer. The outer layer makes more than 30 hormones. They control the amount of salt in your blood. They also help keep the right water balance in your body. If you have swollen joints, hormones made by the adrenals provide some relief.

The inner layers of the adrenals make a hormone called **adrenaline**. Sometimes this is called the "fight or flight" hormone. In times of sudden fear, pain, or anger, your body makes adrenaline. This hormone makes your heart beat faster, releases more food stored by your liver, increases your sweating, and makes you breathe faster. It also speeds up your metabolism.

Imagine walking down a dark street at night. You are alone, and you hear footsteps behind you. They are coming faster and closer, and you want to run away. Your adrenals release more food and let you use that food quickly. Your heart beats faster so the food is rushed to all the parts of your body very quickly. Your breathing increases so you have plenty of oxygen. Your body is getting you ready to run fast. You have probably never run faster in your whole life! Thanks to the endocrine system and the adrenal glands, you are able to get away and make it home safely.

The Pancreas

The next important gland is called the **pancreas**. This gland is found behind your stomach. You might remember learning about the pancreas when we discussed the digestive system. Part of the pancreas makes enzymes that are sent into the small intestine to help break down your food.

The pancreas is also an endocrine organ because it makes hormones. One of the hormones made by the pancreas controls the amount of glucose in your blood. Another hormone, called **insulin**, allows the glucose to move from your blood into your cells. Remember that your cells must use the glucose in the process of respiration to release energy. Insulin lets the glucose move into the cells so it can combine with oxygen and give you the energy you need for everyday activities.

Sometimes a person's body does not make enough insulin. Without insulin, glucose stays in the blood. Remember when we talked about the urine sample your doctor wants from you? If the urine sample shows that you have glucose in your blood, the doctor may treat you for a disease called **diabetes**. You may have to be careful about the kinds of foods you eat. You may have to have medication or shots of insulin to keep you healthy.

Pituitary Gland

The **pituitary** is a small gland, about the size of a marble. It is found at the base of the cerebrum. Sometimes this gland is called the "master gland" because it releases hormones that control other glands in the body. One hormone made by the pituitary is the human growth hormone, **HGH**. This hormone controls how fast your bones, muscles, and organs grow. It determines how tall you will be when you are an adult. The pituitary gland also controls activities of the thyroid, the adrenal, and the reproductive glands.

The Endocrine System

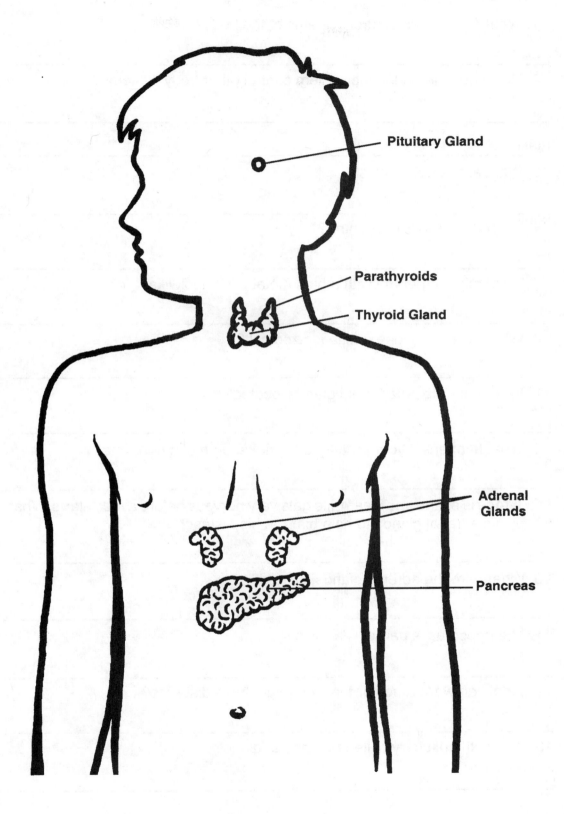

Pituitary Gland

Parathyroids

Thyroid Gland

Adrenal
Glands

Pancreas

Name: _____ Date: _____

Questions

1. What are the two control systems of the body?

_____

2. How does the endocrine system control other body systems?

_____

_____

3. What are target tissues?

_____

4. What does thyroxine control?

_____

5. What might a person with a high metabolism look like?

_____

6. Why is it a good idea to use iodized salt?

_____

7. Where are the parathyroid glands located?

_____

8. What happens if your parathyroids make too much hormone?

_____

9. Tyrone is on the track team. He gets very nervous before a race starts. What is released by his adrenal glands to help him run his fastest?

_____

10. Where are the adrenal glands located?

_____

11. The pancreas is part of what two systems?

_____

12. What can warn a doctor that you might have diabetes?

_____

13. Why is the pituitary called the master gland?

_____

_____

A Graphic Organizer: The Endocrine System

GLAND	LOCATION	CONTROLS
Thyroid	throat	metabolism
Parathyroids	behind the thyroid	calcium and phosphate
Adrenals	on kidneys	salt, water, swollen joints, "fight or flight"
Pancreas	behind the stomach	glucose in blood and cells
Pituitary	at the base of the cerebrum	"master gland"; growth

Activity for the Endocrine System

1. Make a life sized outline of the human body on a large sheet of paper.
2. Draw, color, and cut out life-sized models of the following endocrine glands.

Thyroid	about the size of a bar of soap
Parathyroids	about the size of peas
Adrenals	about the size of lemons
Pancreas	about the size of a banana
Pituitary	about the size of a marble

3. Place the endocrine glands in the proper places on the human body outline.
4. On one set of colored index cards, write the names of the five glands.
5. On another set of differently colored index cards, write the job of each gland.
6. Give the students opportunities to match the name cards to the glands and to match the function cards to the glands as well.
7. Be sure to discuss how the hormones made in each of the glands are able to get to the target tissues.

Research Activities

Assign students to research the following disorders of the endocrine system. Ask the students to present a description of the condition and its symptoms. Have them research the causes and the most recent methods of treatment.

Diabetes	Dwarfism	Gigantism
Goiter	Hyperactivity	

Answer Keys

Getting it All Together (pages 4–5)

1. O	11. T
2. T	12. S
3. O	13. T
4. S	14. S
5. S	15. O
6. O	16. S
7. S	17. S
8. S	18. O
9. O	19. O
10. O	20. O

21.

cells
  tissues
    organs
      systems

22–24. Answers will vary.

A Closer Look At A Human Cell (page 7)

1. Cell
2. Nucleus, nuclear membrane, cytoplasm, cell membrane
3. Nucleus - controls cell activities, controls reproduction, and contains genes
   Nuclear membrane - holds material inside nucleus
   Cytoplasm - contains organelles
   Cell membrane - controls the movement in and out of cell
4. Movement of particles from an area with many to an area of few
5. Special diffusion for fluids
6. Mitochondria
7. Transports materials in the cytoplasm
8. Ribosomes and endoplasmic reticulum
9. A scientist who studies cells
10. Activity—Diagram of a cell
a. Nuclear membrane
b. Nucleus
c. Mitochondrion
d. Vacoule
e. Ribosomes
f. Cytoplasm
g. Endoplasmic reticulum

The Framework: The Skeletal System (page 10)

1. It provides the shape and support for the body like the wooden framework provides shape for a house.
2. It protects them from the environment.
3. The brain, heart, and lungs
4. If you were to be hit or fall, the skull might not be strong enough to protect you completely. Helmets add the necessary extra protection.

5. It works with the muscular system.
6. To give shape and support, to protect organs, to move the body with the muscles
7. A "blob" of muscle, etc., that would have no form and would not be able to move

A Factory and a Storehouse (page 12)

1. It makes blood cells.
2. It stores minerals such as calcium, and it stores fat cells.
3. Calcium is found in many dairy products, and it may be added to orange juice. It is also included in multivitamins and antacid tablets.
4. Answers will vary.
5. Answers will vary.

The Thigh Bone's Connected to the … (page 14)

1. Minerals, protein, water, and living cells
2. About 206
3. Marrow, cancellous (spongy) bone, compact bone, periosteum
4. Flat - ribs, shoulder blades, breast bone
   Long - arms, legs, fingers
   Short - wrists, ankles
   Irregular - vertebrae, ear bones
5. Flat bones
6. Long bones
7. Short bones
8. They give bones their strength and hardness.
9. It gives bones their flexibility.
10. Blood vessels

What's in a Name? (page 16)

1. Skull
2. Jaw bone
3. Collar bone
4. Shoulder blade
5. Breastbone
6. Rib
7. Upper arm bone
8. Lower arm bone
9. Lower arm bone
10. Wrist bones
11. Hand bones
12. Fingers or toes
13. Backbones
14. Hip bones
15. Thigh bone
16. Knee cap
17. Lower leg bone
18. Lower leg bone
19. Ankle bones
20. Foot bones

What's the Connection Here? (page18)
1. Stretchy tissue that connects bone to bone
2. So the bones can work with the muscular system to move the body
3. Tough tissue that protects bones
4. Ends of bones, end of nose, tops of ears
5. It absorbs shock where bones meet.
6. To absorb shock and reduce friction when the spine is moved
7. Protect bones, shape the body, and provide flexibility

What Kind of Joint Is This? (pages 20–21)
1. A place where bones meet or where cartilage and bones meet
2. Fixed, pivot, hinge, gliding, and ball-and-socket
3. Fixed: skull, pivot: neck, gliding: wrist, hinge: knee, ball-and-socket: hip
4. Fixed because it does not allow much movement so it is more solid to protect
5. Gliding, pivot, hinge, ball-and-socket (refer to #3 to see how each move)
6. Fixed
7. The joint is not fixed yet and the brain can be exposed to injury
8a. Pivot, b. Fixed, c. Gliding, d. Ball-and-socket, e. Hinge

Who Are You and What Do You Do? (page 26)
1. Osteology: the study of the structure and functions of bones
2. Ossify: to change or develop into bone
3. Osteopath: a doctor who practices osteopathy, which places special emphasis on the interrelationship of the musculo-skeletal system to all other body systems
4. Osteoporosis: a bone disorder characterized by a reduction in bone density accompanied by increasing porosity and brittleness
5. Orthopedic surgeon: a surgeon who deals with the treatment of deformities, diseases, and injuries of the bones, muscles, etc.
6. Orthotics: the science of developing and fitting surgical devices designed to activate or supplement a weakened or atrophied limb or function

Moving Along: The Muscular System (page 31)
1. Muscle cell
2. Actin and myosin
3. Slide past each other when a muscle is working
4. To stay alive
5. Tell the muscle when to work and what to do
6. More than 650
7. About 30 pounds

8. About 48 pounds
9. No, they have not fully developed control of their muscles, so they aren't as massive as teenage muscles

Do You Want To or Not: Classifying Muscles (page 33)

1. V	6. I	11. V
2. I	7. V	12. V
3. V & I	8. V	13. I
4. V	9. V & I	14. V & I
5. I	10. V & I	15. V & I

What Kind of Muscles Are Those? (page 35)
1. Voluntary and involuntary
2. Voluntary
3. You would have to think about everything you did, including making your heart beat, breathing, and moving food through the digestive system.
4. Because most of the time you do not control blinking, but you can if you want to
5. Skeletal or striated muscles
6. Answers will vary.
7. Autonomic nervous system
8. They are thin and look like spindles with the nucleus in the middle of the cell.
9. Answers will vary.
10. In your heart

Holding It All Together: Tendons (page 38)
1. Two places; one at each end
2. The end of the muscle that does not move
3. The end of the muscle that can move
4. Ligaments attach bone to bone and tendons attach muscle to bone
5. Because the muscles get shorter and thicker when they contract, pulling on the tendons
6. A swollen, sore tendon
7. A ligament, muscle, or tendon that has been pulled (stretched) too much
8. To stretch muscles, tendons, and ligaments gently so they will not get injured

What Kind of Job Do You Have? (page 40)
1. The skeletal system
2. The muscular system
3. People have different muscle tone depending on age and muscle use.
4. Using the muscles too much
5. They are less active and use their muscles less.

Which Way Are You Going? (page 43)
1. Muscles are contracting; getting shorter and thicker
2. Relaxing

3. Messages come from the brain through the nerves

4. Because they contract so quickly

5. Pushing materials through passages, removing materials from body parts, making body openings larger and smaller, contracting and restricting tubes inside the body

6. It is the effect of blood moving through blood vessels.

7. At your wrist or in your neck

8. 70

What's in a Name? (page 46)

1. Lowers arm
2. Catches breath, turns upper body
3. Moves jaw
4. Straightens knee
5. Turns head
6. Rotates thigh
7. Raises upper arm
8. Straightens arm
9. Bends arm
10. Straightens hip

What's Your Problem Now? (page 48)

1. A painful muscle contraction
2. Another name for tetanus; a sustained muscle contraction
3. A bacterial infection
4. A spasm; a series of rapid, repeated involuntary muscle contractions
5. A muscle that has pushed through from its normal position
6. By doing surgery
7. Your muscles need calcium to work properly.
8. Cardiac muscle
9. It shapes and defines them.
10. Your muscles need time to relax and rebuild.

It's Time to Deliver: The Circulatory System (page 52)

1. The paper boy delivers newspapers to all the houses on the route and the circulatory system delivers food, water, and oxygen to all the cells in the body.
2. The missed cell would die.
3. A garbage truck picks up wastes from the houses on its route, and the circulatory system picks up wastes from the cells in the body.
4. The wastes are carried to other parts of the body where they are removed from the body.
5. The wastes would build up and possibly kill the cells.
6. The system in the body that delivers food, water, and oxygen and removes wastes from the body cells

The Little Things You Do (page 54)

1. The blood is very close to the surface, trying to help cool off the body.
2. The blood is farther away from the surface, trying to save heat for the body.
3. To help the circulatory system keep the right body temperature
4. The circulatory system will fight off infections and disease.
5. The medicine helps the circulatory system fight off the disease or infection.
6. They are carried by the circulatory system.
7. The circulatory system carries it there.
8. It carries the medicine to parts of the body where it is needed.

Parts of the Circulatory System: Have a Heart (page 57)

1. DUB (false)   11. DUB
2. LUB (true)   12. DUB
3. LUB   13. LUB
4. LUB   14. LUB
5. DUB   15. LUB
6. DUB   16. DUB
7. DUB   17. LUB
8. DUB   18. LUB
9. LUB   19. DUB
10. LUB   20. LUB

Activity (Labeling Diagram) (page 58)

a. Pulmonary valve
b. Right atrium
c. Tricuspid valve
d. Right ventricle
e. Aorta
f. Pulmonary artery
g. Left atrium
h. Mitral valve
i. Aortic valve
j. Left ventricle
k. Septum

Parts of the Circulatory System: Tubes and More Tubes (page 60)

1. Tubes that carry the blood around the body
2. Three: arteries, capillaries, veins
3. To carry blood away from the heart
4. Connect the arteries and veins
5. To carry blood back to the heart
6. Capillaries are thin enough to let them through.
7. Near the heart
8. With valves
9a. Artery, b. Capillaries, c. Vein

Parts of the Circulatory System: Blood Is Thicker Than Water (page 63)

1. Twelve pints or six liters
2. plasma
3. water
4. dissolved food
5. wastes
6. Red blood cells, white blood cells, platelets
7. red blood cells
8. oxygen, carbon dioxide
9. bone marrow
10. hemoglobin
11. spleen, lymph nodes
12. germs
13. antibodies
14. clot
15. fibrin
16. calcium

What Type Are You? (page 65)

Karen can receive blood from Susan, Nan, Alan, and Barb.

Joanne can receive blood from Barb.

Food For Thought: The Digestive System (page 71)

1. For energy, to build new cells, and to repair body parts
2. You would feel weak and you would not have much energy.
3. Your body would not be able to make new cells or repair itself. You would die.
4. We cannot make our own food, but must eat plants or other animals as food.
5. Answers will vary.
6. Basketball: constant running, shooting, dribbling
Volleyball: serving, passing, hitting, etc.; less than basketball because there is minimal movement, players wait for ball to come into play, and still may not have to move or touch the ball
Reading: arms are being used to hold the book and turn the pages, eyes move
Sleeping: body systems are active, but all body systems slow down
7. The faster a person is growing, the more food the person needs. Children grow much more than adults.
8. It is the process that breaks down the food we eat into a form that body cells can use.
9. It breaks it down so the body cells can use the food.

We Want This to Be as Simple as Possible! (page 73)

1. The physical changes that happen to the food we eat and the physical movement of the food through the digestive system
2. The chemical changes that happen to the food we eat
3. M(echanical)
4. M
5. C(hemical)
6. M
7. M
8. M
9. C
10. M
11. C

The Five Connected Parts of the Digestive System: Activity (page 76)

LABEL DIAGRAM:
a. Mouth
b. Esophagus
c. Stomach
d. Large intestine
e. Small intestine

1. They do not have teeth, or their teeth are not strong enough to break down hard foods.
2. You need small enough pieces to fit into the esophagus comfortably.
3. Moving food around in the mouth, tasting food, help in swallowing
4. The grape has more moisture, making it easier to swallow.
5. 2 pints = 1 quart; 4 quarts = 1 gallon. It would take four days.
6. The movement created by contracting and relaxing muscles in the digestive system
7. The mixture of food and juices found in the stomach
8. The names are talking about organ width. The small intestine is narrower than the large intestine.

Distant Relatives: Organs That Help the Digestive System (page 78)

Activity: Three Diagrams

a. Parotid glands
b. Sublingual glands
c. Submaxillary glands
d. Liver
e. Gallbladder
f. Bile duct
g. Pancreas
h. Pancreatic duct

Like A Breath of Fresh Air (page 83)

1. Several weeks, because the body can store extra food

2. Several days, because your body can store some water

3. There is no way to store extra oxygen in the body.

4. All organisms exchange gases with their environment.

5. To pass oxygen from the air to the blood and to remove gaseous wastes from the body

6. The blood needs to carry the oxygen to all the body cells.

7. The blood picks up the wastes from the cells and carries it to the respiratory system.

8. There is no oxygen in space, so they must carry oxygen with them in the helmets to help them breathe.

9. People and trees are living organisms, so they must exchange gases with their environment.

10. Humans do not have any way to remove the oxygen from the water; they also do not have a way to keep water out of their respiratory systems.

Who "Nose" What the Parts of This System Are? (page 87)

1a. Air sacs

 b. Nose

 c. Tiny hairs

 d. Throat

 e. Voice box

 f. Windpipe

2. Warm the air, filter the air, and moisten the air

3. Your mouth is not able to clean the air as well as your nose can.

4. Because some dirt might get past the nose, especially if you breathe through your mouth

5. To hold it open so you can get the supply of oxygen you need

6. Just use a small amount of air passing through them

7. One leads into each of your two lungs.

8. An upside down tree with the branches becoming smaller and smaller with clusters of balloons on the ends of the smallest branches

9. The oxygen moves from the alveoli into the capillaries that surround them.

10. Inhale: down, contracted; Exhale: up, relaxed

What Is Breathing? (page 89)

1. Taking in oxygen

2. Removal of waste gases

3. The diaphragm, the chest muscles, the ribs, and the breastbone

4. The diaphragm, the chest muscles, the ribs, and the breastbone

5. The air pressure decreases.

6. The air pressure increases.

7. Air naturally moves from an area with greater pressure to one with less pressure.

8. Inhale: 20.9 percent; Exhale: 16.3 percent

9. The body uses some of the oxygen.

10. Your body does not use the nitrogen.

Respiration: What Is It? (page 91)

1. In body cells

2. The digestive system breaks down food to form glucose that is needed for respiration.

3. It carries the glucose from the digestive system to the cells and then carries away the carbon dioxide produced during respiration.

4. Glucose and oxygen

5. Energy

6. Carbon dioxide and water

7. $C_6H_{12}O_6 + 6O_2 \longrightarrow$ (energy) and $6CO_2 + 6H_2O$

8. Breathing, circulation, respiration, circulation, breathing

9. You cannot inhale as much oxygen, so there is not as much oxygen available to combine with glucose to release energy.

10. Yes, a good supply of fresh oxygen is very important to keep a body healthy.

Respiration Activity #3 (page 93)

The lime water should turn white from the students exhaling into the tube. Carbon dioxide causes the change.

You Can't Keep it All: The Excretory System (page 97)

1. C

2. S

3. R

4. C/E

5. D

6. S

7. S/M

8. E

9. R/E

10. M

11. Large intestine

12. Lungs

13. Through the urinary system and skin

The Urinary System (page 100)

1. Kidney, ureters, bladder, urethra

2. To clean the blood

3. The nephrons

4. Your body will produce extra urine to keep everything balanced.

5. To move the urine from the kidneys to the bladder
6. So that it can expand as it stores more urine and then return to its normal size after the urine has passed out of the body
7. The urethra carries it from the bladder out of the body.
8. The kidneys, the ureters, the bladder, and the urethra
9. Some days you drink/take in more liquids, and/or sometimes you sweat more.
10. They cannot control the muscle that releases the urine from the bladder.

What a Waste/Kidney Failure (page 102)
1. To do some tests to see if there are problems inside the body
2. You are in good health.
3. You might have diabetes.
4. You might have kidney problems.
5. You might have injured part of your urinary system, or you might have a urinary tract infection.
6. Two
7. The other kidney will do the work for both of them.
8. You might need dialysis.
9. The patient gets a new, healthy kidney.
10. c. Her sister, because she would have the closest tissue match

That's No Sweat! (page 103)
1. They both remove water, salts, and urea from your blood.
2. It measures your body temperature so you do not become too hot.
3. Because sweat is made up of water, salts, and urea
4. The salts and urea stay on your skin after the water evaporates.
5. Their body temperatures are higher and they need to lower their temperatures.

Keeping it All Going: the Nervous System (page 108)
1. To control the homeostasis of the body
2. The nervous system
3. Seeing, hearing, smelling, touching, tasting
4. It controls your learning and memory.
5. The central nervous system
6. The skull protects the brain, and the vertebrae protect the spinal cord.
7. The peripheral nervous system because they are outside the brain and spinal cord
8. It provides immediate reactions to the environment.

Are Nerves Really Made of Steel: Activity (page 109)
a. Axon
b. Dendrite
c. Nucleus

She's A Real Brain! (page 110)
1. CBR   6. CBR
2. CBL   7. CBL
3. BSM   8. BSM
4. CBR   9. CBR
5. CBR   10. CBR

Ouch! That's Hot! Reflex Action: Activity Graphic Organizer (page 111)
Organizers will vary, but should include the following steps.

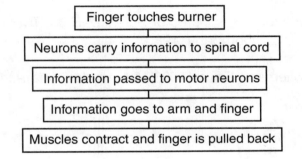

It Takes A Long Time: The Endocrine System (page 116)
1. The nervous system and the endocrine system
2. With hormones that move through the blood
3. The areas where the hormones do their work
4. Metabolism
5. Very thin, even though the person might eat a lot of food
6. The thyroid gland must have iodine to work properly.
7. On the back of the thyroid
8. Bones can become brittle and break easily.
9. Adrenaline, the "fight or flight" hormone
10. On top of the kidneys
11. The digestive and the endocrine
12. Sugar in your urine
13. Because it controls the activities of other glands

Bibliography

Biggs, Daniel, and Ortleb. *Life Science.* Peoria, Illinois: Glencoe/McGraw-Hill, 1997.

DiSpezio, Linner-Luebe, Lisowski, Skoog, and Sparks. *Science Insights: Exploring Living Things.* New York: Addison-Wesley Publishing Company, 1996.

Frohse, Brodel, and Schlossberg. *Atlas of Human Anatomy.* New York: Barnes and Noble Books, 1961.

Gottlieb. *The Wonders of Science: The Human Body.* Austin, Texas: Steck-Vaughn Company, 1986.

Hackett, Moyer, and Adams. *Science.* Toronto: Merril Publishing Company, 1989.

Heimler. *Principles of Science, Book Two.* Columbus, Ohio: Charles E. Merrill Publishing Company, 1983.

Microsoft Encarta '95. *A Complete Interactive Multimedia Encyclopedia.* 1995.